Discovering the
HUDSON

Things were a lot different in the Broadway theater district in 1903 when this shot was taken. Notice no cars or taxis and the tall building on the right, which used to be the Hotel Girard, is still standing along with the Hudson.

Discovering the
HUDSON

New York's Landmark Theatre
From Broadway's Beginnings to
Live Television, Jack Parr, and Elvis

By Ward Morehouse III

Discovering the Hudson
by Ward Morehouse III
© 2007 Ward Morehouse III
All rights reserved.

No part of this book may be reproduced in any form or by any means, electronic, mechanical, digital, photocopying or recording, except for the inclusion in a review, without permission in writing from the publisher.

www.Bearmanormedia.com

1-800-566-1251 (Order line only)
ISBN10: 1-59393-080-1
ISBN13: 978-1-59393-080-6

Printed in the United States

Cover and book design by Bob Antler,
Antler Designworks

Published in the USA by

Bear Manor Media
PO Box 71426
Albany, GA 31708

Contents

Preface   7
Acknowledgements   11
Introduction   13

Chapter **1**
    Broadway's Golden Era Begins   15

Chapter **2**
    "A Brilliancy Never to Be Forgotten"   29

Chapter **3**
    American Drama Comes Into Its Own   38

Chapter **4**
    Harris and the *Titanic*   44

Chapter **5**
    Carrying On   49

Chapter **6**
    Enter George M. Cohan   58

Chapter **7**
    Hot Chocolates, Louis Armstrong, Dutch Schultz and Moss Hart   67

Chapter **8**
    When Radio Was King   76

Chapter **9**
    The Strange Case of Mr. Breen   83

Chapter **10**
    Comedy and Drama Return to the Hudson   96

Chapter **11**
    Live TV, Kate Smith, *Steve Allen's Tonight Show* and Elvis   104

Chapter **12**
    Jack Paar   115

Chapter **13**
    Strange Interlude: Broadway Returns Again to the Hudson   124

Chapter **14**
    "Titanic II" Avoided: Hudson Saved From
    Wrecking Ball   127

Chapter **15**
    Ron Delsener Rocks the Hudson: Music Impresario
    Breathes New Life Into the Theater   132

Chapter **16**
    Harry Macklowe Buys the Theater
    and Builds a Hotel   135

Chapter **17**
    Chairman Kwek   139

Chapter **18**
    Restoring a Landmark   150

Chapter **19**
    Looking to the Future, Theatre Museum, Plans   160

Chapter **20**
    Epilogue   165

Appendices

Appendix A	Findings and Designations	168
Appendix B	Designation by the Landmarks Preservation Commission of the Hudson as an Official Landmark	170
Appendix C	Productions at the Hudson	175
Appendix D	List of Guests on *Steve Allen's Tonight Show*	213
Appendix E	One Thousand and One Events	215

Index   218

Preface

This book is a serious departure from most theater biographies. About people much more than a building, it's an attempt to capture living photographs of an era, beginning with the turn of the last century to the present day in the early part of the 21st century. The Hudson, which was 103 years old in 2006 could have figuratively gone down like the *Titanic*. But it made it, not so much by not closing but because of why it didn't close. This was living theater, theater as romantic and alive as the plays on its celebrated stage.

When I lived at the Lambs Club from 1966 to 1973, at 130 West 44th Street, the Hudson Theatre seemed a forlorn place. I was working at the *New York Post*, sometimes at night during what is called the "lobster shift," from midnight to 8:00 a.m., and going to school at Columbia University working on a degree. This was several years before Ron Delsener renovated the theater and brought a certain respectability back to it with big bands like Count Basie and Miles Davis, stars like Peter Allen, Roberta Flack and Carlos Santana and rock bands of every kind. Back then, 44th Street between Sixth and Broadway was tawdry to put it mildly. During this time, the house manager of the Belasco, who lived at the Lambs, asked me several times if I had seen his "show" at the Belasco. The show was *Oh! Calcutta!* and I thought to myself, "Why should I see that show when I see the ones in the street every night? For free!"

The late developer Seymour Durst once told me hookers who used a ramshackle hotel at Sixth Avenue would chase him down the street when they saw him coming. They had no desire to see him "improve" the Times Square area. Nevertheless, Durst persevered, tearing down an old hotel to make room for another Durst high-rise. Today, his son Douglas Durst, a big supporter of the theater, has changed the map of Times Square while preserving some of its best history—like the façade of the Henry Miller Theatre on 43rd Street behind which he is building an entirely new, state-of-the-art theater.

Anyway, I became a newspaperman in earnest after leaving the Lambs, joining *The Christian Science Monitor* in Boston for four years before coming back to New York as a New York correspondent for the paper. Somewhere along the line, I wrote a play based partly on some of the folks I had met at the Lambs, a play called *The Actors*. It ran for nearly nine months during the 1986-87 season Off-Broadway after getting a nice review from *The New York Times* critic Frank Rich. Little did I know then that a book I would write on The Plaza, called *Inside The Plaza, an Intimate Portrait of the Ultimate Hotel*, would lead me back to the Hudson Theatre, a place which I could tell was full of ghostly memories, a place I never got to know while at the Lambs—even though it was just across the street. This may seem odd to out-of-towners, but every New Yorker knows the sensation of noticing something on his or her block for the very first time—a block they've lived on for thirty years. An historian could spend a career researching almost any block in town. While researching my own book on The Plaza Hotel, I got to know its far-sighted co-owner, Kwek Leng Beng, today chairman of the parent company of Millennium Hotels and Resorts (Millennium & Copthorne Hotels), which owns the Broadway Millennium Hotel and adjacent Hudson Theatre which it restored so beautifully.

Thinking back on it, I realized the Hudson has always "been there". Back in the early 1960's, about the same time *Strange Interlude* was playing at the Hudson with Ben Gazarra and Jane Fonda, my father and I used to go to the Blue Ribbon Bar and Restaurant right next door to the theater. Known for their German pancakes and bratwurst, it was one of the many Times Square landmarks, along with Rector's and Shanley's (and Shraft's, and you name it), which have long disappeared. Broadway was, of course, a different world back then, when Hollywood was still a sleepy train stop somewhere in Southern California. Right down the block from the Hudson, in fact, was the headquarters of Warner Brothers. And Rector's, on 44th Street and Broadway, must have been where the Paramount Theatre building is today—without the theater (but with Planet Hollywood).

Certainly for its first few decades the Hudson thrived in a very colorful time and section of town. According to playwright LindaAnn Loschiavo, gangster Owney Madden, not especially famous for his spiritual side, often found his way to West 45th Street during 1928 to communicate with the unquiet dead. Before performances of *Diamond Lil* at the Royale Theatre, the actress Mae West was fond of holding séances in their smoking room to channel Rudolph "The Sheik" Valentino and tenor Enrico Caruso. Participants included speakeasy owners Texas and Tommy Guinan.

Ms. Loschiavo also informs us that in "1912 Mae West was featured in *A Winsome Widow* and did a ragtime song and a cooch number" at the nearby New York Theatre on 44th Street. On 45th Street, bootlegger Larry Fay ran several speakeasies with Texas Guinan. Also on 45th Street was the Gaiety Theatre Building which housed many African-American music publishers. Mae West loved to perform black-inspired songs and was a frequent visitor to those offices.

Had I known then all that had happened at the Hudson—although I was vaguely aware that a somewhat peculiar theater manager lived above the marquee, in the theater's "apartment," in a rather peculiar housing arrangement—I would have thought of it very differently. But that's Manhattan. The natives run around all day living their hectic lives, pursuing their work, like employees in a gigantic museum, never stopping to ponder the great exhibits they're forever hurrying past.

The Hudson is, along with the New Victory, New Amsterdam and Lyceum, one of the last remaining theaters built before 1920. For sheer drama and anecdotes, on and off stage, it just may be the most interesting and colorful theater on Broadway. The Hudson's story is a little like New York City's itself: a great institution that almost went under during the financial stresses, and social deterioration, of the 1970's. Now, like Times Square, like Broadway, like Manhattan, it's back, revitalized for a new century, maybe even for a new millennium. But I'll let you decide all that, as the curtain is about to go up on a stage that in its time played gracious host to all three New York mass media of the past century: Stage, Radio and Television.

Fancy Rock Island
St. Lawrence River
Thousand Islands
May 2007

THE PLAYBILL

HUDSON
THEATRE

Acknowledgements

I first want to thank my family for creating an environment where theater was an integral, if not intimate, part of our lives. I went to the theater with both my father and mother. With my mother I saw Boris Karloff as Captain Hook in *Peter Pan*, and several years later, Mary Martin as Peter in the musical version. When I was a teenager, my mother, who was co-editor and co-publisher of *The Theater Information Bulletin* and later *Theater Critics Review*, gave me many tickets to Broadway and Off-Broadway shows. My stepfather, Roderic Rahe, loved going to the shows and encouraged me to go as well.

Like many journalists, my first desire was to be a playwright. I thought, as so many young writers do, that given time I could weave my own version of *The Glass Menagerie* or *Long Day's Journey Into Night* from out of hot, thin air and my own life. I had some early success with a play called *The Actors*, which Frank Rich said "demonstrates a flair for flavorful, well-paced comic dialogue and a keen command of the love and spirit of a vanished Broadway era."

Like dozens of other playwrights, I'm grateful to those who gave me the chance to put on my plays and write about theater for many newspapers. I list in no particular order the editors, critics, theater managers, directors, press agents and others who have helped me as a reporter for *The Christian Science Monitor* and as a columnist for Reuters, the *New York Post, The New York Sun, amNewYork,* TimesSquare.com and *Travel Smart Newsletter*. They include the late Curt Sitomer, the American news editor of *The Christian Science Monitor*, who took great joy in fitting people to a particular "best". In my case it was in New York City. Others who have been helpful and who I've admired along the way include: Richard Watts, long-time critic of the *New York Post*; Chuck Caruso and Lou Calisauno, early colleagues at the *Post*; Clayton Jones, John Hughes, Earl Foell and others from *The Christian Science Monitor*; Matt Diebel and Vincent Musetto of the *Post*; Gary Shapiro, "Knickerbocker" columnist of *The*

New York Sun and Seth Lipskey, its editor, as well as Stuart Marques, formerly of the *Post* and the *Sun*; Alex Storizinski, former editor-in-chief of *amNewYork*, as well as Emily Hulme and Marcus Barum.

To Stewart Lane, my collaborator on *If It Was Easy*, and his actress producer wife, Bonnie Comley, I owe special thanks for their always exciting Broadway news and friendship. Publicists Gail Parenteau who represents the Ohies, Beck Lee, Tony Origlio, Barbara McGurn. No list of acknowledgements will be complete without mentioning the hotel executives who have encouraged me to write about the history and glamour of their illustrious establishments, including Kwek Leng Beng, Executive Chairman of The Hong Leong Group which owns Millennium Hotels; Per Hellman, Vice-president and general manager of the Broadway Millennium Hotel, former general manager of The Waldorf-Astoria; Paul Underhill, former asset manager of The Plaza; the late Eugene Scanlan, general manager of The Waldorf-Astoria; Gary Sweikert, former general manager of The Plaza; Tom Civitano, former vice president of public relations and marketing of The Plaza; and Martin Riskin and George Lang, who epitomize both the excitement and promise of grand hotels and their often equally grand restaurants and banquet facilities. Special thanks to Craig Rosenthal, Anne Chubbuck, John Grimaldi, Dina Pinos, John Nania, Robert Dilenschneider, Nadia Ghattas, Jared Pearman and others who have assisted me in writing about the theater and its history. And to Elizabeth Morehouse and William Morehouse, my son, who will know the theater of the next half century.

Introduction

The Hudson Theatre opened on October 19, 1903. Eighteen presidents, two world wars, the Great Depression and countless plays and world events later, its Tiffany glass and elegant Greco-Roman motif which have long dazzled critics and playgoers alike have been restored to their original luster.

Just like the great river that flows majestically not far away from it, the Hudson Theatre began with a man named Henry. "The legend of the Hudson Theatre begins with Henry B. Harris, a St. Louis-born producer," a Broadway Millennium Hotel press release intriguingly begins. "Born into a theater family, Mr. Harris quickly became established in the business, managing his own stars and producing his own plays by his mid-thirties." In 1900, Harris moved to New York where he continued managing and producing and began planning a theater home for himself and his productions.

Over the next nine years, this Hudson Henry either presented or produced forty plays, from the hit *Brewster's Millions*, which ran 163 performances, to a flop called *A Blot in the 'Scutcheon*, which struggled along for five nights. After several years Harris bought out his partner and then opened two more playhouses. He was also director of the Theater Managers' Association of Greater New York, treasurer of the Actors' Fund of America, and the president of National Producing Managers of America.

Harris himself perished aboard the *Titanic* in 1912 but his legacy of championing American plays lived on with his widow, Irene (who was also called Renee) Harris, who became a gifted producer in her own right, and in his theater, which is as beautiful today as on the day it opened. The drama that was so much a part of the Hudson Theatre, both on stage and off, continues. The theater has been not only a symbol of the Times Square renaissance in the latter part of the 20th century but a crown jewel example of Millennium Hotels and Resorts' dedication to landmark restoration.

1

Broadway's Golden Era Begins

As Ethel Barrymore poised on the brink of new romance in *Cousin Kate* at the Hudson Theatre, the first Broadway production to open north of 42nd Street, Eleanor Roosevelt became engaged to Franklin Delano Roosevelt and work began on Grand Central Station, designed by McKim, Mead and White. The great transportation nexus was completed ten years later in 1913. The Wright Brothers, meanwhile, in late 1903, made the first successful, sustained, controlled flight of a powered heavier-than-air craft at Kitty Hawk, North Carolina.

The year just before the Hudson opened steel king Andrew Carnegie moved into his $1 million "cottage" on Fifth Avenue and 91st Street. Twelve years later, it would be overshadowed by one 20 blocks down the street at Fifth and 71st Street: the block-long Florentine palace built by Henry Frick, Carnegie's one-time partner. By the time Frick moved in, spending the last five years of his life there, the structure had cost him some $17 million which he then furnished with some $30 million worth of art.

When the Hudson opened in 1903, Times Square may have been a shadow of its current 21st century high-rise self but it had already been transformed from its lazier days as Longacre Square. The term "The Great White Way," which became synonymous with the Broadway theater, actually had its rather modest origin in 1901 at Broadway and Twenty-Third Street when an electric sign was used to advertise a popular resort of the time. The Hudson also joined a kind

Herald Square used to be New York City's theater capital, as George M. Cohan's song, "Give My Regards to Broadway" refers to when it says "Remember Me to Herald Square." But when the New York Times moved to 42nd Street and Broadway the Broadway theater community moved to 42nd Street and eventually to Columbus Circle and Lincoln Center. DRAWING BY GLYN LEWIS

of land-locked Coney Island of entertainment and eateries which included the indomitable "lobster palaces" where theatergoers gorged themselves on five-pound lobsters and baseball-sized shrimp. The greatest of these was Shanley's. At one time there were four Shanley's in Manhattan including two in what became the Times Square area.

Actually, six Shanley brothers introduced lobster palace society to New York during the "Gay 90's." Shanley's Restaurants were also historic first test cases for music copyright infringement and violation of the Volstead Act. They won the first battle but would lose the second.

According to Robert C. Shanley, former chairperson of the Hotel Division of the Culinary Academy of New York and a direct descendant of Tom Shanley, who in 1896 negotiated a lease with the Astors for the premises on the east side of Broadway and 42nd Street:

"Such an early move was considered bold and risky. The gamble paid off and the success of the third Shanley's Restaurant opened the floodgate for theaters, restaurants and hotels to open in the area soon to be renamed 'Times Square'.

"The fourth and largest Shanley's opened in 1912 at Broadway between 43rd and 44th Streets in the Putnam Building [where the Paramount Building stands today]. This luxurious eatery was complete with cabaret, dance hall and full orchestra. The interior was of plush, lavish décor including glittering crystal chandeliers. The sale of alcohol was an essential factor in defraying the costs of running such an operation.

"Shanley's shared a unique relationship with the early theaters and hotels nearby such as the Hudson Theatre and the Knickerbocker Hotel. Many guests staying at the Knickerbocker would drink and dine before a show at the Hudson and then retreat to Shanley's during the late evening hours. This included a virtual *Who's Who* in the world of theater, entertainment, politics, publishing and high society.

"Famous public figures included President Woodrow Wilson, then-Governor Teddy Roosevelt, the Goulds, the Vanderbilts, the Sloanes, George M. Cohan, Victor Herbert, David Belasco, Charley Delmonico, and Augustin Daly. Legendary wild west lawman turned sports reporter William 'Bat' Masterson was also a Shanley's regular.

"Renowned performers and entertainers included Enrico Caruso, Lillian Russell, Anna Held, Maxine Elliot, Victor Moore, Fay Templeton, Christie MacDonald, Ethel and Maurice Barrymore and Ada Rehan. Jazz music publisher Irving Mills got his start in the music business as a page boy at Shanley's which gave him his first exposure to the theater world.

"Shanley's had a full orchestra that played the classics and show music from all the theaters on Broadway. Shanley's introduced the 'entrance,' where the current stars of theater would arrive after a show. On cue, the orchestra would then strike up the song associated with the star. The crowd would stand and give a rousing round of applause.

"Victor Herbert, the great Irish composer who produced the musical play *Cinderella Man* at the Hudson Theatre, was a regular at

Shanley's. He was also a crusader for the rights of songwriters. While dining at Shanley's in 1913, Herbert was shocked to discover the orchestra playing a number of his works. Herbert and other composers of the day such as Irving Berlin objected to restaurants playing music of living composers without compensation. A four-year lawsuit ensued, until it reached the Supreme Court, which ruled in Herbert's favor. This was a landmark test case for ASCAP and music copyright.

"Congress enacted the Volstead Act in 1919 and Prohibition went into effect January 17, 1920. Shanley's on 42nd Street was the first restaurant to be raided by federal agents under the Volstead Act. This Shanley's closed in 1925. Shanley's on Broadway and 43rd to 44th Streets closed in 1922.

"Restaurateur Peter Shanley, one of the six brothers, was later manager of the Hotel Commodore Bar in the late 1930's. He was now in his twilight years and the only brother still working. Peter Shanley stated in 1936: 'Times Square is misnamed. It was the Shanleys that discovered it and led the way to its prosperity. It should be called Shanley Square.'

"Although I am a direct descendant of the Shanley brothers through my grandmother, my grandfather worked at a Shanley's Restaurant in the late 1890's. He must have anticipated the demise of lobster-palace society with the approach of Prohibition. He took safer refuge in civil service and joined the New York City Police Department. Ironically he would assist in police raids on speakeasies and restaurants and battle the other crime and corruption that Prohibition produced. Patrick Shanley retired as a detective first-grade."

In another postscript, the building housing the original Shanley's at 29th Street and Broadway is still standing but is now a condominium residence. That same building was also once the ultra-fancy Gilsley House Hotel which was frequented by Diamond Jim Brady and theater and opera stars.

The Hippodrome, or simply "the Hippo" as many called it, opened two years after the Hudson in 1905. A forerunner of Madison Square Garden, it was a cross between the old Castle Garden Theatre, built in 1812, where Jenny Lind performed in 1850, and Madison Square Garden. "Its productions," Lewis Hardee notes in his history of the nearby Lambs Club, "featured lavish scenery, spectacular effects, and

Interior of Hudson theater in 1904. MUSEUM OF THE CITY OF NEW YORK

huge casts—as many as five hundred in the chorus. Horses dove into a huge tank at the apron of the stage. Hovering over its mammoth stage huge dirigibles fought 'The Battle in the Skies.' One hundred authentic Sioux Indians sitting in wagons paraded up and down the streets of New York stamping their feet and beating tom-toms, drawing crowds into the theater for the spectacle *Pioneer Days*. Sharing the stage with his fellow tribesmen and one hundred cowboys was William Sitting Bull, the famed chieftain's only son. Pairs of lovers sang 'Moon, Dear' sitting in huge crescent moons high above. Mississippi steamboats appeared on the horizon; legions of soldiers re-fought the Crusades. Giants, dragons, kings, and girls sang and danced."

Playwrights Howard Lindsay and Russel Crouse, who wrote *Life*

With Father, led a syndicate which bought the Hudson in 1943. Lindsay claimed the theater was named for his father, Hudson Lindsay, born aboard ship on the Hudson River. Whether this is true or not, 44th Street, where the Hudson Theatre stands, is arguably the greatest theatrical street in the world today. On this street alone are the Hudson and Belasco (and the Lambs Club Theatre which was a prominent Off-Broadway house before it closed), then the Shubert, Broadhurst, Majestic, Helen Hayes Theatres, the St. James and Minskoff, as well the Nokia Rock Theatre.

Four Times Square theaters actually opened in the same month of 1903: the Hudson, Lyric, New Amsterdam and New Lyceum Theatres.

The New Amsterdam Theatre was completely restored by Disney after the 'House of Mouse' announced it was taking over the theater in early 1994. I was working for Reuters News Service at the time and actually broke the story that Disney was going to announce its takeover of the theater at a press conference that day. Like the Hudson, according to historian Hugh Hardy, much of the success of the renovation of the New Amsterdam was due to artisans who worked on the theater. Missing sections of terra-cotta and plaster were made in molds to approximate those elements that survived. Its original colors of yellow, mauve, green and gold were recreated and signs of the much more flamboyant light musical fare which once graced its stage compared to the more muted colors of the Hudson.

The Hudson, east of Broadway like the Belasco on the block near Sixth Avenue, and the Lyceum, its neighbor on 45th Street, were more or less isolated from other Broadway playhouses. They were neither on Broadway nor on 42nd Street. Moreover, unlike the ornate Lyceum, the Hudson blended almost seamlessly into the row of townhouses it was flanked by. Time, the Depression, and the 1960's with its culture of war, drugs and freewheeling sex, took huge tolls on the Broadway theater district. But the Hudson and its close neighbors were palpably part of the magic of Broadway: frayed around the edges, fading like an old matinee idol by day, shining with light both mystical and magical at night.

The Lyceum is Broadway's oldest continually operating legitimate theater. Built by producer-manager David Frohman in 1903, it was purchased in 1940 by a group of producers that included George S.

Kaufman and Moss Hart. In 1950, the Shuberts took ownership of the theatre, and have operated it ever since.

Widely considered a crown jewel of New York's playhouses, the Lyceum has staged new plays, revivals, and repertory companies since its inaugural production, *The Proud Prince* (1903). Other early shows include J. M. Barrie's *The Admirable Crichton* (1903), *The Other Girl* (1904) with Lionel Barrymore, *A Doll's House* (1906) with Ethel Barrymore, and *The Thief* (1907) with Margaret Illington. Stars of the Lyceum's early years include Fanny Brice, Billie Burke, Humphrey Bogart, Walter Huston, Judith Anderson, Leslie Howard, and Bette Davis.

In the 1940's and 1950's, the Lyceum's biggest hit, *Born Yesterday* (1946), was launched with Judy Holiday and ran 1,642 performances, the theater's longest run. Other productions during this era display the Lyceum's broad scope of dramatic interests, as well as its knack for picking talent: Kaufman and Hart's *George Washington Slept Here*; Clifford Odets' *The Country Girl* (1950) with Uta Hagen; *A Hatful of Rain* (1955) with Shelley Winters; *The Happiest Millionaire* (1956) featuring Walter Pidgeon; Alan Bates in John Osborne's *Look Back in Anger* (1957); Shelagh Delaney's *A Taste of Honey* (1960) with Angela Lansbury and Joan Plowright; and Harold Pinter's *The Caretaker* (1961) with Alan Bates, Robert Shaw and Donald Pleasance.

A number of repertory companies have called the Lyceum Theatre home, starting with Frohman's own company and later the (APA)-Phoenix Repertory Company which produced *You Can't Take It With You* (1965), *The School for Scandal* (1966) and *The Cherry Orchard* (1968). Tony Randall's National Actors Theatre mounted more than a dozen shows here. Lincoln Center Theatre has also staged productions of *Our Town* (1988), *Rose* (2000) starring Olympia Dukakis, Tom Stoppard's *The Invention of Love* (2001), and *Mornings at Seven* (2002).

The Lyceum has also played host to other types of stage presentations such as one-person shows like *Whoopi Goldberg* (1984, 2004 revival), a tour de force which helped launch Goldberg's successful film career; *Ian McKellan: A Knight Out at the Lyceum* (1994); Julia Sweeney's *God Said "Ha!"* (1996); *Mandy Patinkin in Concert* (1997); and most recently the Pulitzer Prize- and Tony Award-winning *I Am*

My Own Wife (2003). But the premieres of new plays have also continued in recent years, including Athol Fugard's *Master Harold...and the Boys* (1982) with Danny Glover, Harvey Feinstein's *Safe Sex* (1987), and Martin McDonagh's *The Lonesome West* (1999).

The Lyceum was designed in the Beaux Arts style by architects Herts and Tallant. The building boasts a handsome gray limestone façade with six ornate Corinthian columns. The foyer sports two grand staircases leading to the mezzanine and marble à la "the marble of Athens." When it opened, the theater featured an early central-air system; the auditorium was kept cool in the summer and warm in the winter by air passing over either ice chambers or steam coils on its way into the theater. Above the theater Frohman built an apartment for himself with a small spyhole door overlooking the stage below. Legend has it Frohman waved a white handkerchief out the open door to tell his wife, the actress Margaret Illington, that she was overacting. The apartment now houses the Shubert Archive.

While it is generally assumed the Lyceum is Broadway's oldest continually operating legitimate theater, the Hudson has the distinction of being the first theater to have a play open in it north of 42nd Street. The Hudson, some of those who in recent years worked to restore it believe, was also the first Broadway playhouse to be fully "electrified."

Construction started on the Lambs Club at 130 West 44th Street in August 1904. A year later the neo-Georgian style clubhouse designed by Stanford White opened, with an ornate 350-seat theater built into its third and fourth floors.

"The location of the new clubhouse could not have been more ideal," writes Hardee in his book on the Lambs. "It was smack-dab in the middle of the new theater district. By 1905 only a handful of theaters remained below 42nd Street, and the theater district having abandoned the area near the former 36th Street clubhouse. Across 44th Street from the Lambs were the Hudson and Belasco Theatres. The huge Olympia Theatre was but a half block away. Across Broadway to the west rose the Astor Hotel, the splendid Belle Époque 'living room of Times Square.' The Broadhurst, Shubert, St. James, and Majestic Theatres also would soon open on West 44th Street. To the east on Sixth Avenue between 43rd and 44th Street was the fifty-three-hundred seat Hippodrome.

"Moreover, the new site was on Clubhouse Row, home to such prestigious institutions as the New York Yacht Club, the Harvard Club, and the Hotel Algonquin [at which the Algonquin Round Table was another kind of club of actors and writers]. Delmonico's, where the Lambs had been founded many years before, had likewise followed the theater crowd and was now located an easy stroll away at Fifth Avenue and 44th Street."

The Lambs held its annual "gambol," or fund-raising show, at the Hudson in 1918, and some of the proceeds went to America's World War I war effort. It was one of many things Renee Harris, Henry Harris's widow, did for the Lambs, a club where her late husband was an honored member.

During the 1950's, I went to many shows with my mother. On weekends I also went with my father, a renowned theater critic, to matinees, sometimes only staying a half hour at each show before moving on to another. We would sometimes stop at the Lambs Club where I'd have a sandwich and my father a drink. Broadway was booming and, according to Lewis Hardee, big time actors were still on the rolls of the Lambs Club—Fred Astaire, Raymond Massey, Al Jolson, Joe E. Brown, Bert Lahr, Danny Kaye, Robert Taylor, Louis Calhern, Spencer Tracy, Charles Coburn, Eddie Bracken, Howard Lindsay, Pat O'Brien, and Ed Wynn. In addition there were important writers, producers, composers, scenic designers, press agents, and librettists. The laity included such celebrities as financier Barnard Baruch, boxing champion Gene Tunney, television czar David Sarnoff, and auto magnate Walter O. Briggs, Jr.

Dr. Randolph Ray, Rector of the Little Church Around the Corner and a paid-up life member, frequently lunched at the Lambs Club. Critics were barred—with critic Ward Morehouse the exception. My father, you see, had been "grandfathered" in as he had been a playwright when he was elected.

During my almost seven years living at the Lambs from 1966 until 1973, the grand old club was, like the rest of the city, in a decline. I think one of the reasons I wrote my first play, *The Actors*, about it and its inhabitants was to capture this great old world of theatrical New York before it evaporated. The old-time actors performing in it, including Richard Waring who co-starred in *The Corn is Green*, loved

This drawing of Ethel Barrymore appeared in the old New York Sun for a story my father wrote on her in his column "Broadway After Dark." Born in Philadelphia, Barrymore, who appeared in the play "Cousin Kate" at the Hudson in 1903 would go on to an illustrious career. The great aunt of film star Drew Barrymore, she died in 1959, 16 years before Drew was born.

the play because it dealt with characters much like themselves in real life. In fact, after several weeks, they took no salary. Their pension and welfare benefits were dutifully paid but they worked for the sheer joy of it. And to hang on to a taste of the world they knew and loved.

Along with the Lyceum, New Amsterdam and the Belasco, the Empire—or at least the façade of it—survives. Built in 1912, the same year as the Cort Theatre on West 48th Street, the Empire was renamed the Eltinge after female impersonator Julian Eltinge. The façade of the Eltinge (aka Empire) was moved west several dozen feet and now serves as the face of the AMC movie complex.

Back on the night of October 19, 1903, there was tremendous activity on 44th Street across from what would be one year later the Lambs Club. Ethel Barrymore, one of the newest stars on Broadway, was opening in *Cousin Kate*, written by Hubert Henry Davies who had achieved a degree of success in London. The play would set the stage for the efforts of scores of American writers whose

This is a rare photo of John Barrmore (5th from left) in "The Forture Hunter," which helped establish him as a Broadway star. He went on to become a silent screen star and costar in some big budget "takies" in the 1930's.

work would be produced by Henry B. Harris and subsequently, after he went down on the *Titanic*, by his widow, Renee Harris.

The commotion started in New Haven. Ethel Barrymore opened in *Cousin Kate* in New Haven on October 12th with an illustrious audience that included the play's producer, Charles Frohman (who later took a special "sleeper" to Syracuse to see a performance, the next night, of Maude Adams in a new play), Ethel Barrymore's brothers, Lionel and John, as well as her uncle, actor John Drew.

The New Haven Register proclaimed in its review that, "The play will succeed. Miss Barrymore is charming in it." Thin on plot, about a spinster who falls in love with her sister's admirer, many critics praised the actress's charm.

Ethel Barrymore began rehearsing for *Cousin Kate* in August. She had seen the light comedy in England and wanted to do it in New York. But the play only lasted a mere six weeks at the Hudson. She then took it on the road where she gained more fame. When *Cousin Kate* left Boston, the great English actor Sir Henry Irving was on his farewell tour in the title role of a play called *Louis XI*. "I had never seen it and I very much wanted to see him die in it so one night I dashed over to the door of the Colonial Theatre, and they let me in," she wrote in her autobiography *Ethel Barrymore: Memories*, published in 1956. When she finally saw him backstage, she lamented that the critics "say I look all right and I have this and that and the other, but that I am always Ethel Barrymore." Irving, Barrymore relates, "put his long, delicate hand on mine and said, 'See to it that they never say anything else.' Those words have carried me through all the years. No notice ever made me miserable again."

Ethel Barrymore opened in *Cousin Kate* at the Hudson the same year her father, Maurice Barrymore, was on stage for the last time. Maurice was as eccentric as he was handsome, and her brother, John Barrymore, inherited both traits in spades.

"I have always regretted that I saw so little of him [her father]," Ethel Barrymore says in *Memories*. "I remember his superlative beauty and how engaging and gay he was, but I heard all the amusing anecdotes about him. ... One of them that I like best is the story of the pompous man who kept saying, 'I'm a self-made man, son, absolutely self-made, son.' Then my father said, 'What happened to you?'

"Sometimes when father was in Philadelphia, he would come to the convent and take me out to lunch, but he could never take me to his hotel because he always lived in terrible ones. He had to, because he always traveled with his animals—a mongoose, a raccoon, and some monkeys and birds—and had to go to some hotel that would take in his menagerie."

Near the end of her memoir, Ethel Barrymore talks of her brother, "Jack" (John) Barrymore and his appearance in *Hamlet* on Broadway. "Of course, I saw him in it many times," she says, "but the most thrilling performance of all was a dress rehearsal just before the opening night. Jack didn't dress for it. He was just in his ordinary street clothes, and I suppose it was the greatest experience I ever had in a theater. It was superb, magnificent, unforgettable, and had in some mysterious way acquired that magical ease, as if he really were 'Hamlet.' It was for me the fulfillment of all I had ever hoped for him and more."

Cousin Kate was actually produced by Charles Frohman, an even bigger theatrical producing giant than Harris. Frohman owned and ran the Empire Theatre on Broadway at 39th Street. Frohman died at sea when the *Lusitania* was sunk by a German torpedo in the Irish Sea before America entered World War I.

Even though *Cousin Kate* had run only 44 performances at the Hudson, the following year Ethel Barrymore was back at the theater in a play called *Sunday* and uttered one of the all-time both classic and silly lines, "That's all there is, there isn't any more."

To another Broadway theater goes the title of "oldest." The Republic, subsequently renamed the Victory and today known as the New Victory, opened on September 27, 1900. As such it is the oldest theater on Broadway followed by the Hudson which opened with *Cousin Kate* on October 19, 1903, then the Lyceum, and later that same year the New Amsterdam.

Along with George M. Cohan and Ethel Barrymore, Minnie Madden Fiske (born Mary Augusta Davey in 1865) was another star from a vanished era to play the Hudson. A star by the time she was sixteen, Fiske had been on stage since she was two years old. Mrs. Fiske (she was seldom called anything but Mrs. Fiske) co-starred in Edward Sheldon's *High Road* opening November 19, 1912, and running 71 performances. "Mrs. Fiske never had beauty but she had magnetism," my father, the late theater critic and historian Ward Morehouse, wrote in his book *Matinee Tomorrow*.

"She had," he wrote, "with all of her nervous, jerky mannerisms, subtlety and finesse, and she was as much at ease in light-handed drawing-room comedy as she was in the problem plays of Ibsen. She was an actress who was eloquent in silence, as demonstrated when she sat for ten minutes without moving and without uttering a word, in the first act of Edward Sheldon's *Salvation Nell*, holding her drunken lover's head in her lap."

Jerry Gross, who helped start the Huntington Theatre in Boston, Massachusetts, says one of the reasons the early 1900's to the 1950's was Broadway's golden era was because "big stars came back to the theater year after year. You have a little of that today. Cynthia Nixon, from TV's *Sex and the City*, is an example of someone with tremendous talent choosing theater. The Lunts, Katharine Hepburn, did it in their day."

2

"A Brilliancy Never to Be Forgotten"

The history of the Hudson properly begins with Henry B. Harris. Born into a theatrical family in 1866 in St. Louis, Harris cut his managerial and producing teeth on road shows and Boston productions before moving to New York and building the Hudson. Before his untimely death some forty plays graced the stage of the Hudson, from *Brewster's Millions*, which ran 163 performances, to *A Blot in the 'Scutcheon*, which limped along with only five. Harris was also active in professional organizations including as director of the Theater Managers' Association of Greater New York and treasurer of the Actors' Fund of America.

After Henry B. Harris went down on the *Titanic*, his father, who had been one of his leading advisors, took over the running of the Hudson and other of his son's enterprises. The younger Harris had such reverence for his father, William, that in the year before his death on the *Titanic* he dedicated the Harris Theatre to him. Actress Rose Stahl was appearing in a play called *Maggie Pepper*. This inscription appeared on the program of the play:

In gratitude to my father, whose influence has shaped my career, I dedicate this theater. Henry B. Harris.

Early in his career William Harris was a member of a song and dance team at DeBarr's Opera House in St. Louis, and then a producer in the Klaw & Erlanger Theatrical syndicate. His son, Henry, would get his first taste of show business selling song books in the gallery. William became an assistant treasurer of the Columbia Theatre in Boston. He then became the business manager of the theater which he ran jointly with Charles Frohman (who went on to produce the first play at the Hudson in New York in 1903) and Charles J. Richard. The first play William produced was *The Widow Jones* in 1894. He made $12,000 on an original investment of $2,500.

Long before playwright Eugene Walter and later, and more dramatically, Eugene O'Neill, would transform American drama from the melodramatic to the realistic, Henry Harris helped set the stage for it by championing American writers. He commissioned Augustus Thomas to dramatize Richard Harding Davis' popular novel *Soldiers of Fortune*. His instincts paid off handsomely, despite a number of flops. The profits from his production of *The Lion and the Mouse* topped a quarter of a million dollars. With these and other earnings he purchased the Hackett Theatre on 42nd Street which was the theater Harris renamed in honor of his father.

It is difficult for modern theatergoers to have a sense of what theater in America (and most of the rest of the world) was like before Stanislavski in Russia and Ibsen in Norway and O'Neill in America started changing it to a "realistic" style. Actually, the one place where you can still get somewhat of a taste of it is in watching old silent films. The wild arm swings, the rather primitive, melodramatic scenarios, the now-painful over-emoting, was what was valued in the late 19th century. Actors weren't supposed to be realistic. They were supposed to be larger than life. The Hudson Theatre's arrival falls more or less on the fault line between the old and the new style in world theater.

While Henry B. Harris was one of the most celebrated producers of the very early part of the 20th century, it was an era of celebrated producers including A. H. Woods, Sam H. Harris, William A. Brady, Sam S. Shubert and, of course, that indomitable showman, Florenz Ziegfeld. After working on the business end of a Boston theater, the younger Harris went on to manage a number of leading stars of the day at a time when box offices both in New York and in theaters on the road were doing land-office business. These stage luminaries

An early Hudson Theatre playbill with picturesque cover

included, among many others, the legendary Lily Langtry.

During a five-year tour of America, Ms. Langtry made a spectacular splash as an actress. Oddly, she had come to acting in London rather late in life and mostly by happenstance. She is probably better remembered in America as an actress than in her home country because she crisscrossed the entire continent, leaving a good impression throughout the states. It is Ms. Langtry, after all, about whom Judge Roy Bean waxed so rhapsodically. She kicked off a cultural awakening almost single-handedly in this country but, when she returned to England, it wasn't long before she retired from the stage.

Eventually owning three theaters on Broadway, Henry Harris saw the Hudson as a sort of semi-permanent home for stars he managed. One of his theaters was the Folies Bergère Theatre, later the Fulton. It's ironic that Harris designed the Folies Bergère, his third Broadway playhouse (built in 1910 and opened in 1911), as a combination theater and restaurant with movable tables in the area where "orchestra" seats are in most theaters—much like the modern-day configuration of the Hudson.

One of the most successful plays Henry B. Harris produced, *The Lion and the Mouse*, was not done at the Hudson at all but at the Lyceum on 45th Street which faced the rear stage door of the Hudson.

Harris may have been loved and respected by many actors but he wasn't perfect. Note the experience of Margaret Illington, a big star of her day. "We went to New London and to the Park Theatre, Boston, where we played for four weeks, selling out," expostulated Margaret

Illington in Ward Morehouse's book *Matinee Tomorrow*. "I asked Mr. Harris about his promise to star me, as I was getting only $200 a week. He finally told me that his father or someone had the bright idea of sending out four road companies, and he would not make me a star because the road companies would not do the play without my having a name. So I had to take the salary I was getting or leave."

Perhaps an irony of the time is that while the acting style and the plays themselves did not do well against the ravages of time, the theaters, like the Hudson, seemed to only grow in charm with age. Virtually alone among the theater artifacts of that earlier era, the theaters have survived and even prospered. You will note that when they meticulously renovated the Hudson, the Ford and other great Times Square area theaters a number of years ago, they neglected to bring back the productions that originally played in them. But perhaps this is always true of drama and architecture. After all, if they had drama in ancient Egypt, it's been long forgotten, but the pyramids endure.

Thus, perhaps it is not surprising that while *Cousin Kate* got mixed reviews, the theater itself got raves. A *New York Times* critic of the era wrote:

> *It is impossible to close without a word of rapture on the new playhouse. Its verde-antique, in Graeco-Roman marble, silk plush and metal trimmings, harmonizes admirably with the dull old ivory of the proscenium arch, picked out with the iridescence of faville glass. The masked lights in the golden house coffers and the moons of opalescent luminaries of the foyer ceiling, the constellations of dull incandescence in the ceiling of the auditorium; all combined to suffuse the house with a rich brilliancy never to be forgotten.*

One wonders if this was standard hyperbolic reportage or whether the gentleman of the press was unusually prescient. Nicholas Van Hoogstraten, in his book *Lost Broadway Theaters*, published in 1991, wrote:

> *Like the foyer, the proscenium arch also had Roman friezes only this time they were copied from the House of Nero. Bay leaf bands and mosaic panels studded with iridescent glass added to its*

unconventional look. The silk velour house curtain of green and yellow matched the muted upholstery in the rest of the theater, which was warmly illuminated by concealed lighting surrounding the stage and direct lighting from small fixtures imbedded in the plaster latticework of the ceiling. The only vivid colors in the auditorium came from Tiffany glass mosaics in the fronts of the balconies and upper boxes.

The design details of the Hudson, and of other theaters of the era, are what most delight and fascinate us today. We have digital lighting, we have audio enhancements for the hearing impaired, we have digitized stage sets, we have acoustical scientists—everything that computers and electricity can provide—but the one thing we can no longer afford in our public spaces is unique, exquisite *objets d'art*. We no longer have the marvelous artisans and craftsmen of earlier ages to fashion those gloriously ornate ceilings, theater boxes, frescoes and other fine embellishments. In some cases, the skills have been lost. Great stonemasons are hard to come by these days. For the rest, it's sadly too expensive now to hire artists to lavish their attentions on one building. The next time you're in downtown Manhattan, stop into the Woolworth Building's lobby (if security precautions these days don't preclude it) and look at the marvelous gargoyles and other bas-relief and artwork. A builder would have to ransom half the collection of the Museum of Modern Art to replicate that ornateness today. This is why we must lavish as much care as we can afford to restore and maintain these great, old, ornate public places like the Hudson. As expensive as it is to repair them, the cost would be prohibitive to reproduce them.

The Hudson's case for restoration was perhaps best presented by the findings of the Landmarks Preservation Commission:

On June 14 and 15, 1982, the Landmarks Preservation Commission held a public hearing on the proposed designation of the Hudson Theatre as an "interior landmark," which would preserve the first floor ticket lobby, inner lobby, auditorium, stage, staircases leading from the first floor to the first balcony floor and all connecting entrance areas. On a more detailed technical and architectural basis, the first balcony floor interior consisted of the first balcony, the upper

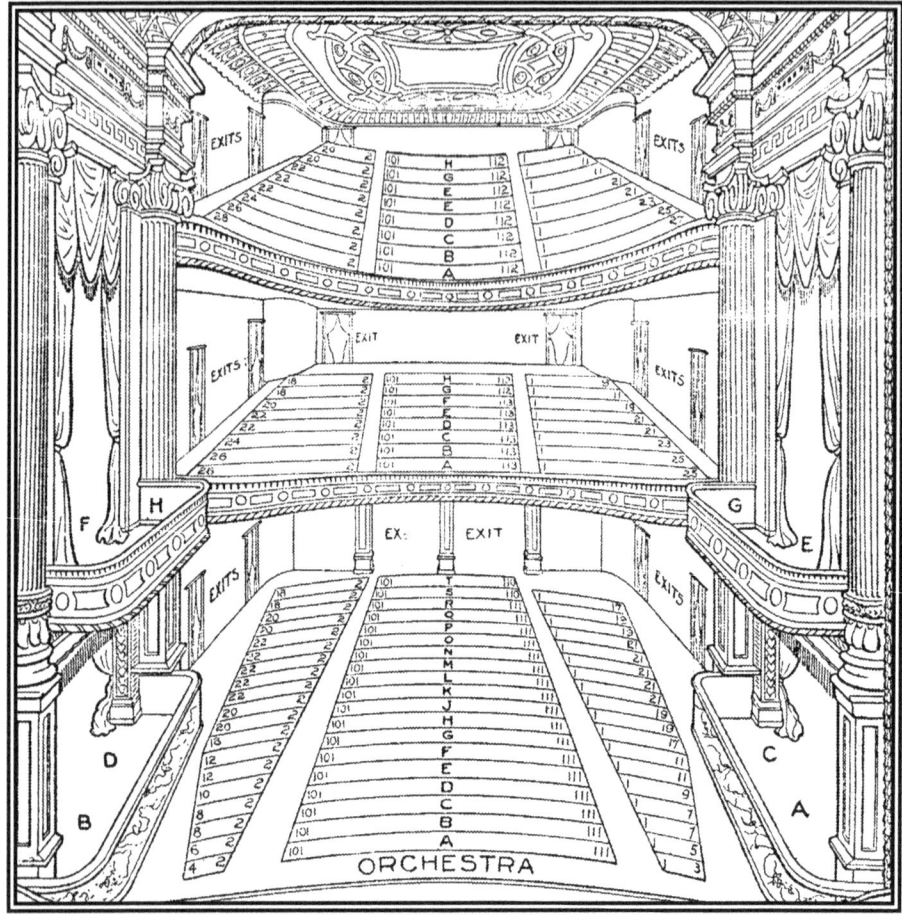

Architectural drawing of seating of the Hudson Theatre in 1909, six years after the Hudson opened. THE MUSEUM OF THE CITY OF NEW YORK

part of the auditorium, the upper part of the stage house, the staircases leading from the first balcony floor up to the second balcony floor and all connecting entrance areas. The "second balcony floor interior" consisted of the second balcony, the upper part of the auditorium and ceiling, the upper part of the stage house; and the fixtures and interior components of these spaces, including wall, ceiling and floor surfaces, doors, stair railings and attached decorative elements. (Even more detail, if you're up for it, can be found in Appendix B.) The commission spent several sessions negotiating what was to be preserved. Eighty-two witnesses spoke or had statements read into the record in favor of the historic designation. Two witnesses spoke in opposition to the designation. Meanwhile, the owner, with his representatives, appeared at the hearing and indicated he had not "formulated an opinion regarding designation." He wasn't sure if the designation was in his best interest, financial or otherwise. If the designation went through, of course, he couldn't alter anything. On the other hand, he would have the glamour and prestige of owning a landmark building. The Commission also apparently received many "letters and other expressions of support in favor of this designation."

The Hudson Theatre's interior is indeed one of New York's historic theater interiors, one that symbolizes American theater for both New York and the nation. Built in 1902-04, the Hudson was part of a burst in theater construction that shaped the character of Times Square as the new center of New York's theater district. Today, it is one of the very few turn-of-the-century theaters in the Broadway/Times Square area.

The restrained exterior of the theater was in sharp contrast to the lavish interior. The exterior's Beaux-Arts classical style blended in with the brownstone houses on 44th Street much like other blocks west of Madison Avenue in the 40's.

The Landmarks Preservation Commission's report on the Hudson's architectural status and landmark worthiness describes the mid-course change in architects and confusion surrounding the change. Architect Craig Morrison says Israels & Harder, the architecture firm of record, were really "the up and coming firm," employing the modern cantilevered balcony construction which needed no support columns. The Commission found that Israels & Harder's work "seems to have included mostly apartment houses, hotels (including the Devon, Walton, Warrington, and Arlington), and commercial buildings, as well as the Turn Verein (1899, 1251-1261 Lexington Avenue, demolished)." Israels had also designed a number of rowhouses in the blocks off Riverside Drive. But the Hudson was the team's only known theater commission, adding yet more support to the building's historic significance.

The mid-course change in architects during the construction of the Hudson led to some confusion in the contemporary architectural press in regards to who deserved the lion's share of the credit for the

Hudson's design. McElfatrick & Son was a prominent firm specializing in theater design, while Israels & Harder designed, as I just explained, no other known theater. Some of the first press accounts attributed the design of the completed theater to McElfatrick, but the plans at the New York Buildings Department are signed by Israels & Harder, and the later press accounts credit that firm, suggesting that the information being made available to the press had been updated. The Hudson bears little resemblance to other theaters designed by McElfatrick & Son, most of which were put up in the 19th century. Even in the 20th century their theater buildings retained much that was typical of 19th century theater design. Long after cantilevered balcony construction had come into common use, McElfatrick was still supporting their balconies with columns underneath, which did not provide great sight lines for those folks behind the pillars. The Hudson Theatre's cantilevered balconies seem to be further evidence that McElfatrick was not the architect. Credit for the final design probably does belong to Israels & Harder.

Harris was as determined to build the finest, most up-to-date theater he could as he was ambitious about presenting shows by authors of promise (in his own estimation, at least). Craig Morrison told me Harris was apparently enthralled with the new cantilevered balconies proposed by Israels & Harder. He approved a change of architects even though the firm which began work on the theater had greater credentials on Broadway. All of a sudden, Israels & Harder were doing the nice, new jobs like the New Amsterdam and the Lyceum, while McElfatrick & Sons, who had been the darlings of theater architects for thirty years, suddenly asked, "what's happened to us?"

The Theatre Museum held an exhibit of ten theaters, "representing legitimate theater architecture in the 20th century," at the National Arts Society Urban Center in early 2007. The theaters on exhibit—the oldest being the Republic (now called the New Victory) and the newest being the "future" Henry Miller on 43rd Street—included the Hudson Theatre

At a time in life when most men do little more than think seriously of retiring, William Harris, inspired by his son Henry's life as well as premature death, backed Bayard Veiller's play *The Fight*, even though he admitted to Veiller he thought he might well take a loss on it.

Veiller called Henry Harris a "distinguished producer of plays." And probably no other tribute could have been greater. The younger Harris also never failed to consult his wife, Renee, about a play. This helped prepare her for her own distinguished producing career, distinguished for its loyalty to talented people as well as to plays by American playwrights in general.

If Henry B. Harris had any counterpart in the latter part of the 20th century, it might have been the late David Merrick, who *Time* in its 1966 cover story called a "phenomenal success." In his biography of Merrick, called *The Abominable Showman*, drama critic Howard Kissel says that Merrick's keenness in discovering English dramas and importing such successes as Tom Stoppard's *Rosencrantz & Gildenstern Are Dead,* Jean Anouilh's *Becket* and Peter Brook's *Marat Sade*, among others, enlightened as well as entertained American theatergoers.

According to Shakespeare, man is nothing but a player who struts about the stage during his time. I wonder what he thought of his theater, the Globe? Did he expect that to endure? Greek drama and Greek theater architecture have survived through the ages. Elizabethan drama, Shakespeare's own, has also passed the test of time. The Globe faded from view for a few hundred years, but it too has been gloriously reconstructed in London. The Broadway theaters of the early part of the 20th century now seem to be making a lasting imprint. One wonders if the heightened melodrama of Joseph Jefferson and Eugene O'Neill's own famous acting father, James O'Neill, will ever return to public favor. If it ever does, the Hudson may well still be there in all its detailed, renovated glory to restage them.

3

American Drama Comes Into Its Own

When the Hudson Theatre first opened to the public in 1903, the American theater still had much to learn from the realistic dramas of Eugene Walter and, in the following decade, Eugene O'Neill beginning with his one-acts such as *The Long Voyage Home*. O'Neill would win a Pulitzer Prize for drama with the production in 1920 of *Beyond the Horizon*. There was Charles A. Taylor's *Through Fire and Water*, described by Gerald Bordman in his book, *American Theater: A Chronicle of Comedy and Drama*, 1869-1914 as a "rearrangement of sensation, melodrama clichés." *Hearts Courageous*, opening at the Broadway Theatre on October 5, 1903, was about a marquis who comes to the American colonies offering them French support against the British. In *Cousin Kate*, Ethel Barrymore played a young woman who doubts that she will ever fall in love. But a chance meeting with an engaging Irishman changes all.

Today a number of theaters east of Broadway struggle to be as successful as their counterparts to the west, and those west of Broadway on 44th Street are booming, including the Shubert and the Majestic.

The Majestic Theatre, where Andrew Lloyd Webber's *Phantom of the Opera* has become the longest-running show in Broadway history running more than 8,000 performances, was also where *The Music Man*, a 1950's megahit, played and the late Jack Lemmon, playing C.C. Bud Baxter in the movie *The Apartment*, waits for Fran, played by Shirley MacLaine, for a date.

This was not the case in the early part of the last century. Then and now those east of Broadway were among the more interesting playhouses. Aside from Henry B. Harris's Hudson, there was David Belasco's Belasco Theatre, just to the east on the same side of the street, and the gargantuan 5,000-plus seat Hippodrome even further east at Sixth Avenue, billed as the largest and costliest theater in the world, built by men who also had Belasco's and Harris's vision and energy. The Hippodrome is long gone but a new Henry Miller Theatre on 43rd Street between Broadway and Sixth Avenue is opening in 2007 with only the landmark's façade left as a reminder of the historical, theatrical past of the original Henry Miller Theatre. (My father's play, *Gentlemen of the Press*, was produced there in 1928.)

By his own admission a "theatrical vagabond," producer-playwright David Belasco, who had trouped the land reciting poetry, dancing, painting scenery and even playing the female role of Gertrude in *Hamlet*, settled down several doors from the Hudson when his very own Belasco Theatre opened in October 1907, the same month and year as the Plaza Hotel fourteen blocks to the north. With murals by Everett Chinn of the "Ashcan School," whose painting of The Plaza also graced it, the Belasco has been the home in recent years of many a hit, including Ralph Feinnes in *Hamlet*. The handsome British actor and film star scored one of his greatest triumphs in *Faith Healer* at the Booth Theatre in early 2006. I was dining at *Un, Deux, Trois*, a restaurant next to the Belasco, when I stayed for several days at the Millennium Broadway in July 2006 and said hello to Feinnes and his dinner companion, Rosemary Harris. Harris had been an old friend of my father's and I have profiled her myself since then.

Born in 1853, David Belasco lived through the Civil War, World War I and the early part of the Great Depression. My father spent many hours listening to the elderly Belasco talk about his days, early and late, in the theater.

My father knew Belasco well and interviewed him many times over the years. "*The Girl of the Golden West* was undoubtedly the play for which Belasco had deepest affection," my father once wrote. "He told me several times that he hoped to revive it, and there were also murmurings from him about *The Return of Peter Grimes*. 'But I tell you, dear Ward Morehouse,' he would say, *The Girl* would go today. I'm going to write Blanche Bates and ask her what she thinks. I'll certainly write her.' I don't believe he ever did." The high point of the play is when blood from the wounded outlaw, hiding in the rafters, drips next to the pursuing sheriff.

Charles Frohman, who opened his Empire Theatre on 39th Street and Broadway in 1893 (the same year the original Waldorf Hotel opened at 34th Street and Fifth Avenue), would have much in common with his neighbor to the north, Henry B. Harris. The location of the Empire at 39th Street and Broadway, coupled with the prestige of its owner, Charles Frohman, helped usher in Longacre Square as the city's new theater center. It had been creeping north for decades, from the Bowery to Union Square before pausing, however briefly, at Madison Square with such playhouses as the Garden, the Lyceum, and the Madison Square.

In another New York theater history irony, Eugene O'Neill was born in a hotel room in Longacre Square in the late 19th century when it was still a pleasant, respectable neighborhood of hotels and houses. Subsequently *The New York Times* moved into the area, as did the theater district from downtown, transforming Longacre Square into Times Square. The neighborhood, needless to say, changed dramatically. Later in life, O'Neill would return to the block on which he was born and grumble about how much the old place had changed. He and his playwrighting had changed it as much as anyone else! Back then, New York City was home to dozens of daily newspapers. The *Times* was prominent but hardly the monolith it has become in recent decades. Perhaps those wily old theater owners knew something. When the *Times* moved to Longacre Square, maybe the theaters moved north to make it easier for the *Times'* play reviewer to make it back to the paper in time to write the review? Or at least, the shorter trip was less likely to make him irritated.

Frohman, who personally treated his actors well, had been part of an alliance of showmen called Theatrical Trust or Theatrical Syndicates which started in 1896 and eventually gained monopolistic control over playhouses in America. Joseph Jefferson, who brought Washington Irving's *Rip van Winkle* to life on dozens of stages across America, generally fought losing battles with the Syndicate. Mrs. Fiske, who would rather fight than play to their tune, found herself featured in skating rinks and everything except a bowling alley.

Talking about the Syndicate in *The Stage in America (1897-1900)*, Norman Hapgood wrote that "its growth was rapid, its power immense...actors like Richard Mansfield spoke large words about his independence, and when the temptation came he ate them." He and other actors of the day tried to counter the influence of the Syndicate by forming one of their own. One by one these actors capitulated to the system. "Mrs. Fiske then stood alone," Hapgood wrote. But he went on to say that, "The power of the syndicate, of which he [Frohman] is the producer head, makes for mediocrity in acting in plays. ... It is doubtful whether, with hundreds of actors to draw from, he could make out on 'Becky Sharp' as well as Mrs. Fiske did. ..."

But Harris and Frohman, who both controlled stars' fates like benevolent puppet masters, fared worse than some of their stars. Harris, of course, went down on the *Titanic* in 1912 and Frohman, along with 1,152 other passengers, on the *Lusitania* three years later. As prescient as they were about playwrights and theater architecture, New York's early 20th century theater operators did not have a similarly great track record when it came to booking transatlantic passages. As much as we worry today about the dangers of jet travel, the skies are still a heck of a lot friendlier than the Atlantic Ocean ever was.

A moment here to give equal time to the benefits of sea travel. Years later, Will Rogers himself would perish in a plane crash during a visit to Alaska. Just think how different New York theater history might be if the industry in the first half of the 20th century has simply had a shrewder travel agent.

On May 11th, 1915, *The New York Times* carried an interview with actress Rita Jolivet that I quote here at some length. It speaks of the extraordinary courage of some of the richest and most famous men who died when the *Lusitania* sank after being hit by a German U-boat.

> "We stood," said Miss Jolivet, "talking about the Germans and the rumor which had gained currency that a man, obviously of German origin, had been arrested for tampering with the wireless. The story was that the man had been discovered at one o'clock in

the morning a day or two before, doing something to the wireless apparatus and had been immediately imprisoned. I did not see the man arrested, so I am not sure about the story's truth, but there were good grounds for believing it.

"We determined not to enter the boats, and just a minute or two before the end Mr. Frohman said with a smile: 'Why fear death; it is the most beautiful adventure that life gives us.'

"Mr. Scott fetched three life belts, one for Mr. Vanderbilt, one for Mr. Frohman, and one for my brother-in-law. He said he was not going to wear one himself, and my brother-in-law also refused to put his on. I hear that Mr. Vanderbilt gave his to a lady, Mrs. Scott. I helped to put a life belt on Mr. Frohman. My brother-in-law took hold of my hand and I grasped the hand of Mr. Frohman, who, as you know, was lame. Mr. Scott took hold of his other hand, and Mr. Vanderbilt joined the row, too. We had made up our minds to die together.

"Then Mr. Frohman, in a perfectly calm voice, said 'They've done for us, we had better get out.' He knew that his beautiful adventure was about to begin. He had hardly spoken when, with a tremendous roar, a great wave swept along the deck and we were all divided in a moment. I have not seen any of those brave men alive since. Mr. Frohman, Mr. Vanderbilt and my brother-in-law were drowned. When Mr. Frohman's body was recovered there was the most beautiful and peaceful smile upon his lips."

The Hudson, meanwhile, continued to have hot plays. One such drama, *The Show Shop*, starring Douglas Fairbank, whose greatest claim to fame would be as a romantic leading man in silent films, opened on December 31, 1914, and ran 156 performances. Then 1916 brought *The Cinderella Man*, a comedy by Edward Childs Carpenter and starring Frank Bacon, to the Hudson stage. It ran 192 performances.

Producer A. (Al) H. Woods brought a light comedy into the Hudson in 1918 with *Friendly Enemies* by Samuel Shipman and Aaron Hoffman. It ran a whopping 440 performances until the later part of 1919. Around the corner at the New Amsterdam Roof on 42nd Street

Will Rogers was giving "Talks on Timely Topics" in what was billed "his last appearances in New York for a year." The show, under the umbrella name of "Ziegfeld's Midnight Frolic," included "30 of the Most Beautiful Girls in America and we can prove it." Over at the Hudson the "Bendix Quartette" played selections from such well known music as *The Star Spangled Banner* and the operas of Puccini between acts.

4

Harris and the *Titanic*

On the evening of April 14, 1912, the Harrises sat down as usual for dinner in the *à la carte* restaurant aboard the *Titanic*, a step below the ritzy superliner's most luxurious restaurant where caviar, quail eggs, and lobster were consumed with Edwardian abandon. "One of the liveliest tables was occupied by the Harrises and the Futrelles," Rick Archbold and Dana McCaulay write in their book *Last Dinner on the Titanic*. "Jacques Futrelle was a successful mystery writer who took great pride in being called 'the American Sherlock Holmes.' Holmes' creator, Arthur Conan Doyle, had been a boyhood hero of Futrelle's."

The Harrises and others in the *à la carte* restaurant had a choice of dining on seven courses, including a third course of Filet Mignon Lili —filet mignon with foie gras and truffles. Mrs. Harris, according to *Last Dinner on the Titanic*, broke her arm only hours before the *Titanic* struck an iceberg. And Captain Edward J. Smith (sometimes called "the millionaire's captain" because of all the ships he skippered that were sailed on by the Astors, Vanderbilts and Guggenheims) stopped by the Harris table to wish her a speedy recovery say the authors of this book. Henry B. Harris and his wife occupied Cabin C-83, paying 83 pounds and 9 shillings.

While Henry B. Harris spent the months proceeding passage on the Titanic planning new productions, John (Jacob) Astor IV and his young bride, Madeline Talmadge Force (who was less than half his age), "enjoyed the luxury of a houseboat on the Nile," according to Justin Kaplan in his book *When the Actors Owned New York*.

The Titanic left on her maiden and only voyage from Queenstown, England on April 11, 1912. She sped past Ireland, striking an iceberg two days later and sliding beneath the icy surface of the North Atlantic in just 2 hours and 40 minutes. Renee Harris had fallen and broken her arm during the voyage. Before the ship went down she put her jewelry into husband Henry B. Harris's pockets. When his body was recovered the jewelry, which was even then valued at many thousands of dollars, was missing. PHOTO BY CORBIS

Not knowing Harris's fate aboard the *Titanic*, this message, a so-called Marconigram, was prepared to be sent to him aboard the *Carpathia* which rescued *Titanic* passengers:

> *Anxiously awaiting news as to how you are; can assist in railroad accommodation if know your condition; ring me on telephone; love to all*
>
> —J. H. Hoadley

With Harris's death, the playhouse, which the *Dramatic Mirror* called "among the handsomest in America," would fall into the fledging, but highly capable, hands of his widow, Renee Harris who, incidentally, later claimed she was the last one to be put in one of the lifeboats.

"I saw him [her husband, Henry] go down," she once told Sidney

Setting the Scene of Broadway's Golden Era ∽ 46

Henry B. Harris (bottom center) was just one of the famous and near-famous people who died on the Titanic when it stuck an iceberg and sank on April 14, 1912.

News of the sinking of the Titanic stunned the world. Broadway producer and Hudson Theatre owner Henry B. Harris was among the 1,500 passengers who lost their lives when the superliner, said to be "unsinkable," struck an iceberg and sank about 400 miles off the coast of Canada's Newfoundland. His widow, Renee Harris, who went on to be a gifted producer in her own right, later said believed she was the last person to leave the sinking ship alive.

Fields for his column "Only Human," which was once an institution in the *New York Daily News*. "It took me two years to get over it. ... The last thing he did was put all my jewelry, $150,000 worth, in his pocket. A lot of the others' jewelry was found. I think whoever found him took his jewelry and put the body back in the water. ... But we had twelve years of supreme happiness. Few people have that. ... I married four times, all told, but I really had one husband—Henry."

Though the jewelry that he had stuffed in his pockets for her was never recovered her indomitable spirit never left her. Someone once asked, "How was this old woman, Renee Harris, to prove that she was the last one off the *Titanic* when it sunk?" whereupon Mrs. Harris, hearing this, tartly responded, "I don't give a hang if I was the last one off or not, but I won't have anyone calling me an old woman!" She was 91 at the time.

Henry B. Harris was dead. The tributes poured in. The *Dramatic Mirror* paid Harris this tribute:

HENRY B. HARRIS

In the melancholy death of HENRY B. HARRIS the American drama loses one of its most consistent and enterprising patrons. Although he never posed as the champion of the native author,

he rarely, either through design or accident, imported his offerings from Europe. Certainly his recent dramatic successes were, without exception, the works of American playwrights.

MR. HARRIS also had the courage of his convictions, for *Strong Heart, The Lion and the Mouse* and *The Third Degree*—with which his name is probably most often associated—each opened up a new theme and won the flattery of imitation. These plays,

moreover, had been refused by other producers, who could see nothing in their possibilities. Because a given subject had not been successfully treated by previous writers apparently never seemed to MR. HARRIS a sufficient reason for refusing to consider it.

Some of his less successful productions indicate the variety of his understanding and the sincerity of his desire to advance the American theater. Among them was *The Christian Pilgrim*, a dramatization of *Pilgrim's Progress*, which pleased an intelligent, but, unfortunately, limited, clientele. Another delightful play which could not find its public was *The Scarecrow,* a whimsical fantasy based on one of HAWTHORNE'S short stories. His most unusual production this year, *The Cave Man,* whatever its defects as a drama, was at least a brilliant satire on contemporary life. In common with the others, it shows MR. HARRIS'S readiness to try the new.

Another novel venture of his was the Folies Bergère, which attempted to combine the somewhat incompatible diversions of the dinner table with the distractions of the music hall. After two seasons this plan succumbed and the building was converted into a theater. The failure, however, left its mark on Broadway in the impetus given to the cabaret shows in neighboring restaurants.

His importance in the theatrical world is indicated by the fact that he owned or controlled four New York theaters, and that in each of them has been produced at least one success this season.

In spite of the influence which he had won by his own efforts, MR. HARRIS remained a man of whom one hears only kindly words both from his business associates and from his personal friends, and that makes his taking off the more grievous.

Just what effect his death may have on the theatrical situation cannot be foreseen. Certainly the American dramatist with new ideas will not find a producer more willing to introduce him to the public than was HENRY B. HARRIS.

5

Carrying On

When Henry Harris went down in the *Titanic*, his touring companies were crisscrossing America, from Waterloo, Iowa, to Hannibal, Missouri; from Bath, Maine, to Wichita Falls, Texas; and from Santa Fe, New Mexico, to Fresno, California. He left an estate which included the Hudson and Harris Theatres, as well as a lease on the Fulton Theatre and the Grand Opera House. He had also leased the Walnut Street Theatre in Philadelphia. In addition to his real estate interests, Harris managed a number of stars of the day including Lily Langtry and Robert Edeson. He also had as many as 18 touring companies during the 1910-11 season, at a time when touring live shows was comparable to owning movie theaters and getting a percentage of the ticket sales today.

But Harris's widow, Renee, also discovered that with all his holdings Harris overextended himself—that he had virtually no solid assets free from debt. The last *HMS Titanic* passenger to get into a life boat which was later picked up by the *Carpathia*, Renee Harris was born Irene Wallach on June 15, 1876.

Mrs. Harris became post-*Titanic* Broadway's first female producer. For one play she produced called *The Noose*, she hired a chorus girl named Barbara Stanwyck. Stanwyck later became a star in *Burlesque*, which Mrs. Harris had encouraged her to do.

She later produced Moss Hart's first play, *The Beloved Bandit*, which critics hated and which closed out of town. Hart was eternally grateful to her for her support, as her belief in his talent led to a meeting with playwright George S. Kaufman and the two men became the most celebrated co-authors in American theatrical history. But despite her financial hardships in later years, Mrs. Harris said, whenever she looked out at the world she loved, "you've been good to me, old boy. I owe you much more than you ever owed me."

Nor was all the high drama happening solely to the Hudson's owners. The theater itself would soon cruise into some rough waters. Bayard Veiller's play, *Within the Law,* had become a huge Broadway hit and vastly increased interest in his subsequent works. But a play of his called *The Fight* shut down the Hudson. Something in this latter play did not strike the New York authorities as being "within the law." Eventually, he and the Hudson would lose "the fight."

"What was drawing the crowds was a perfectly innocuous scene in a house of ill fame," Veiller would recall later in his autobiography *The Fun I've Had.* "People were fighting to get into the theater. And on the fourth night we were all arrested."

William Harris carried on the tradition of his son Henry's graciousness to an extreme. "He was a little [man] with a soul as big ... I think it was as big a soul as anyone ever saw," said playwright Bayard Veiller, who had occasion to test Harris's soulfulness with *The Fight.*

Harris "came down to rehearsals every day just to see the second-act curtain," Veiller wrote in *The Fun I've Had.* "He was very definite about the curtain. 'It's the best second-act curtain ever written,'" Veiller quotes Harris as saying. "And day after day he beamed and crowed and was happy."

Veiller, despite having written it, was of an entirely different opinion. "It was unbelievably bad," he thought. Producer Martin Beck, after whom the Martin Beck Theatre was named (albeit recently renamed the Al Hirschfeld Theatre), told Veiller the trouble: "What you want is a better-looking madam and six prettier whores, and then you have got a hit."

Harris, however, told Veiller he would have produced it just because Harris had told Veiller "so often how good it was."

"What we did," Veiller continued, "was to write an entirely new second curtain the next night, after which we went into New York and opened to big business. And the second night, bigger business. On the third night, Pop [William Harris] offered me fifty thousand dollars for my interest in the play. People were fighting to get into the theater." *The New York Times* carried the following story on *The Fight*, including it with another lurid play called, aptly, *The Lure*.

> To PLAY 'THE FIGHT' IN REVISED FORM
> ----------
> But Waldo Refuses to Pass on the New Version in Advance of Its Production
> ----------
> POLICE WILL BE ON HAND
> ----------
> Shubert Invites Members of the Grand Jury to Pass Upon "The Lure" at a Performance To-night.
> ----------

There will be performances to-night of "The Lure" and "The Fight," the two plays to which the police objected on the ground that they were public nuisances. Lee Shubert, producer of "The Lure," has invited the members of the Grand Jury to attend a performance, and he has sent invitations to others who might be interested in the question of its fitness as a production. "The Fight," produced by the estate of Henry B. Harris, will be revised.

Meanwhile both producers have been released in their own recognizance in accordance with an agreement with Chief Magistrate William McAdoo that the two plays would be withdrawn pending the transfer of the cases from Special Sessions to the Grand Jury.

Max D. Steuer, representing the estate of Henry B. Harris, informed Police Commissioner Waldo in a letter yesterday of the intention of the producers of "The Fight" to give a revised production of that play to-night. He offered to furnish Commissioner Waldo with a copy of the revised version or to have a special performance for him before the regular performance was begun. Up to late yesterday afternoon Mr. Steuer had received no reply from Commissioner Waldo, and he felt, it was said, that the Police Commissioner would take no action to prevent the performance.

Commissioner Waldo said that he would not pass upon the

revised version of "The Fight" before the play was produced. "I will have men who are qualified to pass on the merits of the play at the theater to-morrow night," he said, "and they will report to me. If the play violates the law, I will procure a writ and have the matter thrashed out in the Supreme Court within twenty-four hours. In the event that the decision of the court should be against the play, I will revoke the license of the Hudson Theatre."

When the revised version of "The Fight" is staged to-night, Magistrate McAdoo explained that action against its producers would have to be begun all over again. He was informed that the police would be on hand to pass upon the performance.

The *Times* followed up this story with one that both shows would go on after changes.

> Following the receipt of a letter from Lee Shubert in which he agrees to have "The Lure" rewritten so that all objectionable parts will be eliminated, the Grand Jury, on the recommendation of Assistant District Attorney Bostwick, decided yesterday to drop its investigation which was to determine whether the play was a proper one to present to the public. The investigation of "The Fight" since the play appeared in its new form, also has been discontinued.
>
> The decision to drop the inquiry into the morality of "The Lure" was reached after many conferences between Assistant District Attorney Bostwick, Lee Shubert, Samuel Untermyer, Mr. Shubert's counsel, and Max D. Steuer, counsel for the Harris estate. Mr. Steuer on Monday wrote to Mr. Bostwick to say that "The Fight" in its original form would not be presented again, either in New York or on the road.

By today's standards, in the wake of such "nudie" shows as *Oh, Calcutta* which was presented at the nearby Belasco more than half a century after *The Fight* was featured at Hudson, *The Fight* was tame stuff indeed. The scene that the authorities objected to and over which they shuttered the show was basically a "tableau"—or brief scene—of women in a bordello, most of whom were fully clothed.

The Times Square area certainly has seen its share of ethical sea changes over the course of the past one hundred years. About half a century after the fight over *The Fight*, the area had progressed far beyond being someplace where an innocent young man might see a chaste depiction of a bordello in a play and had become the city's red light district. In effect, the whole place had turned into an actual bordello. It was the whores who were more likely to chase away the policemen than vice versa during the city's downturn in the 1970's. And then the area turned upside down all over again when Disney moved in during the 1990's, transforming the theater district into a wholesome Manhattan theme park of sorts, suitable for all ages.

Friendly Enemies, a play by Samuel Shipman and Aaron Hoffman, came into the Hudson on July 22, 1918, with a cast that included Felix Krembs, Louis Mann and Sam Bernard. It was about two German ex-patriots living in America, both having become millionaires, who differed vehemently on which side was right, Germany or America, in World War I. The play was updated to World War II when it was made into a movie nearly 25 years later co-starring Charles Ruggles, James Craig, Otto Kruger and Nancy Kelly. *Friendly Enemies*, the play, ran longer than its successor *Clarence* (which ran 300 performances) for a total of 440 performances.

A strange fate befell the man, A. H. Woods, who presented *Friendly Enemies*. Mr. Woods did not believe in investing in stocks or even apparently in bank accounts. He put $800,000 in cash in a safe deposit box and eleven years after the successful opening of *Enemies*, when the stock market crashed, he went to retrieve his nest egg only to find the box empty. He could only conclude that his partner, who possessed a duplicate key, must have cleaned him out.

Back in 1918 life was much rosier for Mr. Woods, for the Hudson, and for New Yorkers in general. According to a theater program for *Friendly Enemies*, Church's Cabaret, at Broadway and 49th Street, was offering a "special dinner" for $1.65 with "Dancing on the Main Floor." Meanwhile, over at the New Amsterdam Roof (Theatre), the "Ziegfeld Midnight Frolic" kicked off its performances at 11:30 p.m. Then there was the Electra Chocolate Shop on Fifth Avenue and 36th Street which advertised in the same Hudson play brochure that it sold the "Highest Grade of All Kinds of Chocolates of the Most Delicious Tastes."

Another fairly long running pre-Twenties play at the Hudson was *The Cinderella Man*, a comedy by Edward Childs Carpenter, which opened on January 17, 1916, and closed 192 performances later. Carpenter also wrote the popular play *The Bachelor Father*. Carpenter would die in 1950, the same day as Boston's famed, influential Irish Democrat John Francis ("Honey Fitz") Fitzgerald.

During the 1920's, and with the solid success of rentals as well as her own productions at the Hudson, Mrs. Harris' wealth increased to where she owned a yacht, an apartment on Central Park South, and a country house, among other holdings. She was offered more than a million dollars for the Hudson on the eve of the stock market crash in 1929 but turned it down only to find she actually owed more than $100,000 on the theater.

In turning down that whopping $1.2 million for the Hudson, Mrs. Harris might have submarined her own financial interests but she also may very well have saved the Hudson and the neighborhood for posterity. Her refusal to sell put a bit of a lid on the skyward march of Times Square. It was said that those who offered her that tidy sum wanted to erect a skyscraper on the site of the Hudson. Now flanked by office towers and high-rise hotels, including the Broadway Millennium Hotel and its luxury wing, the Millennium Premier Tower, the Hudson and Belasco on the same block are a welcome relief from the skyward flights around them.

Walter Lord interviewed Mrs. Harris for his celebrated book on the *Titanic* disaster, *A Night to Remember*. He would continue to visit her, even when he said he found her living in a single room in an old hotel, the kind of place that was derided as an "SRO" before the time when even the most run-down hotel in Manhattan seems to have been transformed into appealing if not luxurious living space. But, he said, "she had lost neither her sunny disposition nor her poise.

"One day I brought her a little jar of caviar in an attempt to give this gallant lady a taste of the good, old days. She sampled it at once, then pushed the jar politely aside. 'You call that caviar?' she chided."

But we're getting ahead of our story. The Roaring Twenties brought new excitement to Broadway, as well as a speakeasy or two. The

Alfred Lunt really became a Broadway star in Booth Tarkington's hit play "Clarence" at the Hudson in 1919. He married actress Lynn Fontanne in 1922 and they appeared in over two dozen plays together. They made one movie, "The Guardsman," in 1931.

Hudson was right in the middle of all the fuss. A "Yankee Doodle Dandy," one George M. Cohan, dominated the Hudson; and Mrs. Harris would find that one of her greatest successes was discovering a genuine American genius: Moss Hart.

The 1920's began with a bang at the Hudson. *Clarence*, starring

Alfred Lunt and Helen Hayes, opened on September 20, 1919, and became one of the Hudson Theatre's biggest hits, running for 300 performances. One of the high points of drama was the 1927 production of Sean O'Casey's *The Plough and the Stars*, starring Arthur Sinclair and Sara Allgood. Siobhan O'Casey, Sean O'Casey's daughter, remembered her father's warm recollection of the landmark production. He loved coming to New York.

Clarence by Booth Tarkington proved to be a landmark production in many ways. It opened at the same time the recently-formed Actors' Equity Association called a strike.

Alexander Woollcott opined in his review of the comedy for *The New York Times* that the play was "As American as 'Huckleberry Finn' or pumpkin pie. It is as delightful as any native comedy which has tried to lure the laughs of this community in the last ten seasons."

And it catapulted Lunt to stardom, a fame which he improved upon with the assistance of his equally celebrated actress wife, Lynn Fontanne, for nearly the next half century. The play's great author was so pleased with the cast of the play, and with Lunt in particular, that he waxed ecstatic about their performances in a letter which was pinned to the call board of the Hudson Theatre.

"Please express my gratitude to all of the *Clarence* company," he wrote, keeping far away from the opening night and several performances thereafter, "and tell them to note how nicely a play goes when the author keeps away from it.

"I'd like you to note a certain important thing— even more important than the author's staying away, viz, a cast as well fitted, well acting and personally attractive as this one could play the Telephone Directory and make it a hit.

"If you had got one of those people wrong you could have lost. They made New York dramatic critics face about—the play didn't do that, not for a minute—the cast did it.

"When I wrote *Clarence* I had a pretty accurate guess that Cora was what Helen Hayes needed as proof of her big range, just now—also, there was no Cora without Helen Hayes, of course.

"Please shake Lunt's hand for us."

The play ran some 300 performances before going on tour. Lunt himself brought the same kind of naturalness to the title role of the

Chistine Ebersol (right) and Mary Louise Wilson hold Tony Awards they won in Grey Gardens in June, 2007. They are in Tony d'dNapoli's restaurant in the Casablanca Hotel near the Hudson Theatre. PHOTO BY ROSE BILLINGS

Tarkington play that John Barrymore would display in *Hamlet* a little later in the decade. And, yet, it was one thing to be natural with drama and something entirely different to be natural with comedy which was usually done very broadly. "Ever since he had been a student at Carroll College," Jared Brown writes in his book *The Fabulous Lunts,* "Lunt had experimented with new approaches to acting. In *Clarence* he was able to put some of them to use for the first time in his professional career. For example, there was his theory about the effectiveness of turning his back to the audience during an important moment in the play. In both the first and last acts, Lunt played scenes of dejection with his back to the audience, and his slowly drooping shoulders spoke at least as eloquently as any gesture or facial expression would have. In Act IV, when dejection turned to elation as the letter Clarence had thought would never arrive finally reached him, the audience saw Lunt's back straighten with hope before they saw the expression on his face."

What a remarkable family Henry Harris had. First his father William successfully takes over management of his theater, then his wife Renee. Despite all types of personal tragedy and business setbacks, they stayed true to the theater's noblest maxim: "The show must go on."

6

Enter George M. Cohan

If Henry B. Harris built and ran the Hudson and was married to it as few theatrical producers were with their theaters, then George M. Cohan had an affair with it. The Hudson in the Roaring Twenties belonged to George M. Cohan, also known as the "Yankee Doodle Dandy" and "The Man Who Owned Broadway."

With the partnership of Cohan and Harris dissolved, Cohan in the next eight years virtually lived at the Hudson Theatre. (The Harris that was George M. Cohan's partner was not Henry B. Harris but Sam Harris, a longtime former Cohan partner.) *The Meanest Man in the World* opened at the Hudson in 1920, and it was the first of a remarkable run of shows he did at the Hudson in the 1920's.

In fact, during the 1920's George M. Cohan produced, incredibly, no less than ten shows at the Hudson Theatre. This gives no meaning to the term "Roaring Twenties." For George M. it was rip-roaring when it came to mounting productions of his own and others' shows at the Hudson.

Here, colorfully, authoritatively, and inimitably chronicled by our favorite pop culture author, Chip Daffaa, are those ten George M. Cohan productions that kept the Hudson so busy during the decade:

1. *The Meanest Man in the World*, written by Augustin MacHugh. This play (later turned into a movie starring Jack Benny) opened October 12, 1920, at the Hudson, starring Frank M. Thomas. Cohan himself subsequently took over the starring role. Besides originating roles, Cohan liked slipping into roles created by others. Demand for

George M. Cohan, sometimes called "the man who owned Broadway," may have had many shows at the Hudson in the 1920's, a theater he didn't own, but by the early 1900's he was a millionaire several times over and owned Broadway playhouses himself.

My father's personal friendship with George M. Cohan led to his 1943 biography of the man who is sometimes called America's first show business superstar. The book, "George M. Cohan: Prince of the American Theatre," was published a year after Cohan's death.
Photo by Corbis

tickets would then inevitably increase; Cohan—known as "The Man Who Owned Broadway"—was enormously popular with theatergoers. This play ran 202 performances— a long run in that era. With his first production at the Hudson a big hit (and his own George M. Cohan Theatre then occupied by his long-running play *The Tavern*), it is perhaps not surprising that Cohan kept putting shows into the Hudson. Throughout his career, Cohan demonstrated great loyalty to people and places he liked. (He could be loyal to a fault; as a producer he was occasionally criticized for using too many old friends in his shows, actors he'd worked with in the past and liked personally, rather than finding the best possible new players.) But if his first production at the Hudson was a hit, he was happy to return there with more shows. The

Hudson, of course, was just as happy to have him; Cohan's track record as a producer, not just as a playwright and performer, was good.

2. *Nemesis*, written by Augustus Thomas and starring Emmett Corrigan and Pedro de Cordoba, opened April 4, 1921, and ran for 56 performances at the Hudson.

3. Next, beginning May 23, 1921, Cohan starred at the Hudson for twenty-seven performances of his own great hit *The Tavern* (which, as noted above, had been for the previous six months been running at the George M. Cohan Theatre). Of all the shows Cohan wrote and appeared in, this was perhaps his favorite.

4. Cohan's production of *So This Is London* by Arthur Goodrich, starring Lily Cahill and Edmund Breese, opened August 30, 1922 at the Hudson, and ran nearly a year—357 performances.

5. *The Song and Dance Man*, produced by, written by and starring George M. Cohan in a role inspired by his father. The show opened December 31, 1923, at the Hudson and ran 96 performances. This drama was an important show in Cohan's career, winning him unprecedented critical acclaim as a straight actor. Cohan had first made his mark on Broadway as a brash entertainer, a personality; he more or less just played himself in one early musical comedy after another. Beginning with *The Song and Dance Man* (in which Cohan did not sing or dance), the critics began to acknowledge Cohan's eminence as an actor, capable of portraying with surprising subtlety and conviction, characters other than himself.

6. Cohan next starred at the Hudson in his own rather slight comedy *American Born*, which opened October 5, 1928, at the Hudson and ran for 88 performances; people came to see Cohan—not the play.

7. *The Home Towners* (produced and written by Cohan and starring Robert McWade) opened at the Hudson August 23, 1926, and ran for 64 performances.

8. Cohan next presented *Los Angeles* at the Hudson, written by Max Marcin and Donald Ogden Stewart, and starring Frances Dale and Alison Skipworth; it lasted just 16 performances.

9. Cohan wrote and produced *Whispering Friends*, which opened February 20, 1928, at the Hudson starring Chester Morris; it ran for 112 performances.

10. The final Cohan production to play the Hudson was *By Request*, written by J. C. and Elliott Nugent who also co-starred in it; it ran 28 performances.

George M. Cohan's fondness for the Hudson Theatre was at least indirectly tied to his love of the Lambs Club across the street, some Lambs Club members believe, even though he resigned from the club following the founding of Actors' Equity. Cohan, of course, also had a fondness for the Friar's Club, but the Lambs seemed to be his favorite and the late Henry B. Harris was a prominent Lamb and had once been its treasurer.

The incredible thing is that the shows Cohan presented, one after the other, at the Hudson were only part of his Twenties output. Here is a chronology of other productions Cohan either produced or acted in during this time:

1920 Cohan, as a solo producer, presented a comedy, *Genius and the Crowd*. Cohan also produced *The Tavern* with Arnold Daly in the leading role.

1922 *Madeleine and the Movies*, presented at the Gaiety Theatre with Georgette Cohan in cast. ... *Little Nellie Kelly* with Elizabeth Hines presented at the Liberty Theatre.

1927 *The Baby Cyclone*, farce in three acts by George M. Cohan, Henry Miller's Theatre, September 12. Players included Grant Mitchell, Joe Allen, Nan Sunderland, John T. Doyle, William Morris, Georgia Caine. Cohan appeared in *The Merry Malones*, Erlanger's Theatre, September 26.

1928 Cohan presented *Billie*, a musical version of his own Broadway Jones, at Erlanger's Theatre on October 1; and Ring Lardner's *Elmer the Great* with Walter Huston in the title role opened on September 24 at the Lyceum.

The Song and Dance Man at the Hudson was a critical triumph, as well as a box office smash. Alexander Woollcott, who was a New York drama critic from 1914 to 1928, said he was surprised "to find how deft, how artful, how quiet, how winning and how gently pathetic a comedian is George M. Cohan." About the show itself the testy, fretful and trenchant Alexander Woollcott reviewed *The Song and Dance Man* in the *New York Herald* in 1923:

> The rumor that George M. Cohan was giving serious consideration to the idea of leaving the theater flat [was] effectively disposed of last evening. The latter was attended to at the Hudson, where Mr. Cohan bobbed up engagingly in a comedy dedicated to the proposition that show folks are show folks and so must remain until they die. That is the sum and substance of a scanty new play of his called *The Song and Dance Man* which arrived breathless from Boston just in time to justify the enterprising press agent in case he should want to plaster the ash barrels today with the legend: "Second Year in New York."
>
> The piece is one which Mr. Cohan concocted as a sort of blotter to sop up the spare time of Lynne Overman, the amusing fellow who shared the stage with Vivian Martin during the long, uneventful run of *Just Married*. It is usual in such cases for the actor playing the leading role to vanish from sight after the third or fourth week and thereafter for startled and delighted audiences to find Mr. Cohan himself playing the part. This time, they say the substitution was made in the middle of the first week, and, behold, a pert, hasty, moderately amusing play has become somehow good with this delightful comedian at large in it.
>
> The early George Cohan who bounded about in the days of *Running for Office* and *The Governor's Son* must have made a singularly deep impression, because now, even after many years, it is an annual surprise to find that he is not like that at all—an annual surprise to find how deft, how artful, how quiet, how winning and how gently pathetic a comedian is George M. Cohan.
>
> One calls the new piece hasty, not from any a prior knowledge, but because it does sound as if he had written it on the back of an envelope while he was waiting for the barber. Of course there is no special merit in slow work and the greatest speech of the last two thousand years was written on the back of an envelope [Lincoln's

Gettysburg Address]. But the mere fact that *The Song and Dance Man* makes an agreeable pastime does not conceal the fact that the author has put about as much into it as he would have put into a twenty minute sketch.

"The Man Who Owned Broadway" (Cohan) opened his musical, *The Song and Dance Man*, into the Hudson on December 31, 1923, and the show lasted 96 performances. Business for eight performances, including two shows on Wednesday and a special benefit performance Thursday night, totaled $15,476.00 according to theater records. As you might expect, Saturday night's take was the largest, totaling $2,681.00. Friday night was second to Saturday at $2,189.50. Cohan paid $1,500.00 rental for the theater. Compare that to today's prices which run upwards of $50,000 a week for theater rental.

"As a writer of musical-comedy texts and songs, he introduced a fresh, new manner," David Ewen writes in *American Musical Theater*. "The plays, like their author, were jaunty, swiftly paced, vivacious." "A symbol of brash violence in theatrical entertainment," one critic would write.

"But following the bitter loss in his feud with the Actors' Equity Association in 1919—Cohan opposed its function as a union and wrongly thought many of his fellow actors would line up with him—he began losing interest at least in musicals. He continued writing and appearing in plays, both musicals and non-musicals," Ewen writes. "Two non-musicals [produced at the Hudson] were minor successes: *The Tavern* (1920) and *The Song and Dance Man* (1923). Most of the others were failures. 'I guess people don't understand me no more,' he remarked, 'and I don't understand them.'"

My father's association with the Hudson—and George M. Cohan—started in 1920: "I came North from Atlanta in the late fall of 1919 and in the frigid November of that year I set foot on Broadway for the first time in my life. I met George Cohan in 1920 when he was playing at the Hudson in *The Meanest Man in the World*."

My father wrote this in his biography of Cohan, *George M. Cohan: The Prince of the American Theater*.

When I arrived in New York, with the determination to gorge

myself on big-time drama after devoting years to seeing every road show that came below the Rappahannock, the Broadway theater was rampant. Fifty-odd attractions were available in the legitimate houses. The marquees of the midtown playhouses spelled out their magic wares: Frank Bacon in *Lightnin'*, Fay Bainter in *East is West*, Ethel Barrymore in *Déclassée*, Ina Claire in *The Gold Diggers*, John and Lionel Barrymore in *The Jest*, Edith Day in *Irene*, Helen MacKellar in *The Storm*, Lillien Lorraine in *The Blue Devil*. And this was the theatrical season that also brought forth John Drinkwater's *Abraham Lincoln*, Booth Tarkington's *Clarence* [at the Hudson Theatre] (in which Tarkington proved that he could write a play, and also a part for an engaging young actor named Lunt), Billie Burke in *Caesar's Wife*, and James Forbes' best play, *The Famous Mrs. Fair*, which sent young Margalo Gillmore off to a brilliant start.

The theatrical producers of the time were quite as celebrated as the stars in their productions. They were personalities. They had great prestige and they lived well; they spent enormous sums of money—whether they had any or not. They had expensive homes. They took trips. They went to London, to Paris, to the South of France; to Palm Beach, to French Lick Springs, and continually to Atlantic City for weekends at the shore. On almost any Saturday afternoon the famous Boardwalk presented a managerial parade: George M. Cohan, Lee Shubert, A. H. Woods, Martin Herman, Sam H. Harris, C. B. Dillingham, and the brothers Selwyn, Edgar and Arch. And in New York, if not along the Boardwalk, you found such illustrious fellows as Lincoln A. Wagenhals, Henry W. Savage, Winthrop Ames, A. L. Erlanger, George C. Tyler, Crosby Gaige, John Golden, Winchell Smith, Arthur Hopkins, Collin Kemper and the great Ziegfeld, who wore lilac shirts, collected jade elephants, sent thousand-word telegrams and maintained a zoo at Hastings-on-Hudson, elephants and everything, for the delight of his wife, Billie Burke, and their daughter, Patricia.

It was a day of giants in the play producing field—but their day was passing, and they seemed to know it. And they were having their fun while they could. As the Twenties came along it was apparent that the theater was undergoing startling change. New

Cole Porter, who many believe ranks equally with Irving Berlin as America's greatest songsmith, never had a show at the Hudson Theatre but first made it big on Broadway with his 1929 musical "Fifty Million Frenchmen" at a time when Broadway and the Hudson Theatre were booming. Moss Hart, whose first play "The Beloved Bandit," was produced by Hudson Theatre owner Renee Harris in the mid-1920's (but closed out-of-town) struck Broadway gold with his collaboration with George S. Kaufman on "Once in a Lifetime" in 1930.

careers were taking shape—new producers, new playwrights, new players. The early Twenties were to see the disappearance, the elimination, of some of Broadway's spectacular showmen, just as the new realism was to become the fashion in the drama and a new order of playwrights was to replace such craftsmen as Augustus Thomas, Eugene Walter, George Broadhurst, James Forbes, Avery Hopwood. And as Broadway reached the third decade of the century the sugar-coated play of the George Cohan-Winchell Smith formula was on its way out.

The early Twenties were to witness the sure and steady rise of Eugene O'Neill, the projection of John Barrymore, the development of such players as Jeanne Eagels, Emily Stevens, Helen Hayes, Katharine Cornell, Lynn Fontanne, Alfred Lunt, Holbrook Blinn, Pauline Lord, Tallulah Bankhead, Ruth Gordon. And such dramatists as Maxwell Anderson, George S. Kaufman, Marc Connelly, Elmer Rice, Sidney Howard, George Kelly, and Rachel Crothers who, like Owen Davis, was a holdover from another era.

Aside from his producing responsibilities, Cohan himself took the leading role in 1920 in *The Meanest Man in the World* at the Hudson.

Three years later, on December 31, 1923, to be exact, he took the leading role in his *Song and Dance Man* which my father said, "brought joy into the hearts of the Loyal Order of Cohan."

I think it's interesting that, while much of Broadway was going wild with Prohibition-related activities, the Hudson was in the tamer and more nostalgic-minded hands of George M. Cohan for much of the decade—bravely holding out against the tides rising all around it of café society gone wild. At her speakeasy ten blocks north of the Hudson, cowgirl-turned-silent-screen-star-turned-saloon-keeper Texas Guinan opened her infamous 300 Club with its scantily-clad fan dancers and free-flowing bootleg liquor. George Gershwin didn't necessarily have to fight his way to Guinan's piano but stars who frequented the club were a veritable milky way of celebrity, from silent film heart-throb John Gilbert to Irving Berlin, who lived in a townhouse on West 46th Street near Sixth Avenue for much of the 1920's until the stock market crash wiped out most of his Broadway fortune up to that time.

George M. Cohan is one of the towering figures of American theater. He did, really, as much in his inimitable way to change Broadway as did Eugene O'Neill. The latter brought respectability and deep thought to the New York stage, as well as realistic scenarios and acting. Cohan was at more or less the same time bringing the masses to Broadway. Suddenly regular folk were going to the theater. Sure, Cohan used patriotism and a charming hucksterism to lure them in, but like O'Neill he helped broaden Broadway's appeal. Broadway was becoming truly democratic, a place where almost anyone could find something to their liking. And his favorite theater, the Hudson, like that noble lady in the harbor, was happy to open her doors to all.

7

Hot Chocolates, Louis Armstrong, Dutch Schultz and Moss Hart

I don't know if Woody Allen was inspired by this for his movie *Bullets Over Broadway*, but gangster Dutch Schultz, who invested in *Hot Chocolates* which opened at the Hudson in 1929 and "featured" Louis Armstrong, fancied himself a bit of a playwright. He had told the writer, Andy Razaf (1895-1973), the show needed "a funny number ... something with a little colored girl singing how tough it is to be colored." When Razaf refused, Schultz reportedly pinned him to the wall and put a gun to his head. The songwriter finally did as he was threatened to do and soon found himself seated next to his "collaborator" on opening night. Promisingly, the audience started to laugh then suddenly stopped. Razaf, trembling with fear, was awaiting his fate when Schultz heartily slapped him on the back and congratulated him.

Schultz, the so-called "Beer Baron of the Bronx," born Arthur Simon Flegenheimer on August 6, 1902, in the Bronx, was the former beer truck driver for Arnold Rothstein. Mr. Rothstein, you may recall, was rather famously shot in a hail of bullets in a barber chair at the Park Central Hotel on November 4, 1928.

Of course, before "The Dutchman," as Mr. Rothstein came to be called, met his end, he uttered these less than immortal words in 1935: "I never did anything to deserve that reputation [Public Enemy

No. 1], unless it was to supply good beer to people who wanted it." These words echoed Al Capone's earlier remarks that, "all I ever did was sell beer and whiskey to our best people." Both lines sound like they might make good song lyrics in a Broadway musical.

Armstrong's rendition of *Ain't Misbehavin'* ("I'm saving all my love for you") stole the *Hot Chocolates* show and he recorded it in July 1929. It became the biggest hit of his career up to that time. But even before *Hot Chocolates* moved to the Hudson in 1929, Armstrong had already made a name for himself as a band leader. Okeh Records let him choose the musicals and songs for the recordings, and these 78 rpm records featured Johnny Dodds on clarinet, "Kid" Ory on trombone, and Johnny St. Cyr on banjo while Armstrong's wife, Lil, was on piano.

Before Armstrong came to the Hudson, white theatergoers had to travel uptown to Harlem to 125th Street and 133rd Street, once called "Swing Street" before the name because associated with 52nd Street and its musical revues. By 3 a.m. Harlem's Swing Street was "jumping" as the Fats Waller song, *The Joint is Jumpin'*, put it.

The best and most entertaining authority to listen to on the subject of *Hot Chocolates* and Louis Armstrong is writer Chip DeFaa, who has long covered music and pop culture:

"The groundbreaking revue *Hot Chocolates*—also known as *Connie's Hot Chocolates*—was one of the major black Broadway musicals of the era and an important stepping stone in the careers of songwriters Fats Waller and Andy Razaf and entertainers Louis Armstrong and Cab Calloway. This revue had its start—initially titled 'Hot Feet'—as a high-spirited floor show at Connie's Inn (on Seventh Avenue and 131st Street) which was, along with the Cotton Club, one of the two leading nightclubs in Harlem. Gangster Dutch Schultz, who supplied Connie's Inn with its liquor, bankrolled the transfer to Broadway. Schultz, along with Connie Immerman (who ran Connie's Inn) and Leonard Harper (who supervised the shows there) wanted the Broadway production to be bigger and brighter than the floorshow at the club, which would continue as a late-night attraction there, throughout the show's Broadway run.

"The Broadway production, which opened June 20, 1929, at the Hudson Theatre (after a tryout at the Windsor Theatre in the Bronx),

Trumpet virtuoso Louis Armstrong may not have received star billing in the ground-breaking musical "Hot Chocolates" at the Hudson but its success would help propel him to the very top of his profession and his film and TV appearences made him a household name.

boasted a huge company of 85 performers—everyone from Edith Wilson and Russell Wooding's Jubilee Singers to Jazzlips Richardson and the Six Crackerjacks. Among the artists added to the show for its Broadway run was Louis Armstrong—initially hired simply to play trumpet in the pit band. Armstrong had spent the last five years in Chicago where he had won a following among black audiences and general recognition from jazz musicians as, not just the foremost jazz trumpeter, but the foremost jazz musician of the era; but he was not yet known to the general public. With his appearance in this show Armstrong's general fame was not long coming.

"In a letter to jazz critic Leonard Feather (September 18, 1941), Armstrong recalled his role in *Hot Chocolates*: 'I was the trumpet man in the pit at that time, playing under the direction of the then-famous Leroy Smith. Oh boy—whatta show. In this particular show I used to feature the theme song of the show called "Ain't Misbehavin'." I played this solo during the entr'acte of the show. In other words, I played this tune between the first and second acts. And take it from me, Gate—it was really in there. After I'd finish the show at the Hudson Theater, I'd rush immediately up town and do a show at the Lafayette Theater, up in Harlem, then from there I'd wind up downstairs at the Connie's Inn cabaret.'

"None of the Broadway reviewers singled out Armstrong by name. The only review that even so much as alluded to Armstrong ran in *The*

New York Times (whose critic did not bother to find out Armstrong's name): 'A synthetic but entirely pleasant jazz ballad called "Ain't Misbehavin' " stands out, and its rendition between the acts by an unnamed member of the orchestra was a highlight of the premiere.' Well, yes, it no doubt was a highlight; as countless jazz musicians noted—and recordings confirm—no other trumpeter of the time came near Armstrong's virtuosity. And if Broadway reviewers, for the most part, did not seem to recognize Armstrong's gifts, audiences did, and the producers soon found ways to make more use of him. By July 8th, they had Armstrong coming up on stage to join Edith Wilson and Fats Waller in singing a number, 'My Man is Good for Nothing But Love.' And they found another spot for Armstrong to play 'Ain't Misbehavin',' right after Paul Bass and Margaret Simms sang it as a first-act duet. In November, late in the Broadway run, juvenile lead Paul Bass was replaced by a far more charismatic entertainer—a singer/bandleader (and friend of Armstrong's) from Chicago, Cab Calloway. That show introduced Calloway—who would soon attain fame as a recording artist—to New York.

"Reviews of *Hot Chocolates* were mixed. While the *Herald Tribune* hailed the show as the 'Best Negro Revue Since *Blackbirds*,' and the *Sun* said it had 'the liveliest ensemble to be seen on Broadway,' most reviewers seemed oblivious to the strengths of its score. 'Woefully lacking in tunes,' opined one theater critic; another wrote dismissively: 'the music is just noise arranged for voice and instrument, and played noisily.' The show boasted two numbers that would become enduring standards—two of the best-known numbers that Fats Waller and Andy Razaf ever wrote: 'Ain't Misbehavin'' and '(What Did I Do to Be So) Black and Blue?' Astonishingly, only one reviewer even acknowledged the latter song. *Variety* observed: 'Miss Wilson scored with "Black and Blue" ... quite a lyric.'

"It was indeed quite a lyric. What made *Hot Chocolates* such a groundbreaking musical was 'Black and Blue'—the first song of racial protest by black writers ever to be heard on Broadway; the first song of racial protest ever to become a hit. Dutch Schultz had pressured Andy Razaf to write a comic number for Edith Wilson to sing, about how hard it was to be dark-skinned. Razaf was uncomfortable with the assignment, which he found demeaning; but 'public enemy'

Dutch Schultz was not someone you said no to. The song that Razaf and Waller created, ostensibly to give Schultz what he'd requested was brilliantly—and subversively—written.

"When Wilson introduced the song in the show, audiences had no idea what was coming. They'd been hearing various lighthearted comic numbers. When the lights came up on the hefty, dark-skinned Miss Wilson, dressed all in white, in an all-white bedroom set, they saw only a striking visual contrast of black and white. When she started singing the introduction, about how lighter-skinned gals had better luck getting men than she did, audience members initially laughed, thinking it was going to be just the sort of mock-complaint comic song Schultz had wanted.

"But as she got into the song, the laughter stopped; she was making a bold, forthright statement for equality, which hit audiences hard. She sang: 'Just 'cause you're black, folks think you lack, / They laugh at you and scorn you too. / What did I do to be so black and blue? / When you are near, / they laugh and sneer, / set you aside, / and you're denied, / what did I do to be so black and blue? ... / My only sin is in my skin. / What did I do to be so black and blue?'

"Audiences had never heard anything like it on Broadway. It was not the frivolity they associated with revues, black or white. (It was certainly not what Dutch Schultz had expected; but *Hot Chocolates* was pulling good audiences, so he was satisfied. *Hot Chocolates* was a big success, its run foreshortened by the 1929 Stock Market Crash and the onset of the Great Depression.)

"Louis Armstrong did not get to sing 'Ain't Misbehavin'' or 'Black and Blue' in the show, but he recorded them as the 'A' and 'B' side of a single record that became—in October of 1929—the biggest hit he'd recorded to date, one of the records that helped break him out from the jazz world, helped make him the household name he would soon become. 'Ain't Misbehavin'' and 'Black and Blue' would remain staples of Armstrong's repertoire for the next forty years. And the song 'Black and Blue,' which Broadway critics largely ignored when it was introduced on the stage of the Hudson Theatre, would prove its potency again, some fifty and sixty years later, when it was revived to provide climactic moments in hit Broadway shows."

Harlem in this era was a sort of musical theme park ahead of its time. It also was a place rife with a degree of racial segregation that most New Yorkers would now care to forget. The old, middle-class neighborhood north of Central Park had become the main area for blacks recently migrated from the South to settle in during the early decades of the 20th century, largely because it was of the few places they were allowed to settle in. And it wasn't because the rents were low. Quite the contrary. These new New Yorkers brought with them their rich musical culture, and the city became mad with jazz. Black jazzmen performed at all the clubs, but many of these establishments were for white patrons only. The locals had their own clubs. All of them were jumping, however. Fortunately, the segregation left but the jazz stayed. However, Harlem itself would experience changes similar to Times Square. It would travel through a rough financial period in the '60's and '70's and then have a cultural renaissance in the 1990's.

One of the most notable productions never to have played the Hudson in the late 1920's was Moss Hart's *The Beloved Bandit*, which was produced by Renee Harris. It closed in Chicago without making it to Broadway and the Hudson. But Mrs. Harris' motherly treatment of the budding playwright, who went on to become one of America's foremost dramatists and directors, encouraged him to try harder and smarter the next time. Her spunk and determination to present the playwright foreshadowed efforts to save the Hudson itself in ensuing years. Hart got George C. Kaufman to collaborate with him on his next play. Hart, co-author with George S. Kaufman of some of Broadway's greatest comedies, recounted some of his exploits leading up to and including this production in his autobiography *Act One*. When Mrs. Harris optioned his play, he was still working as an office boy and "my dual career as office boy and built-in playwright swung into full gear," he writes.

"It did not seem at all extraordinary to me that I should go about my duties as office boy in the morning, emerge as playwright in the afternoon, then revert to the role of office boy again at the end of the day: closing the windows, emptying the wastebaskets, stamping the mail and then taking it to the post office on my way to the subway," he wrote.

"Only Mrs. Henry B. Harris seemed to gather a secret amusement from the situation, and she treated me from our first meeting on with a grave outward courtesy that was belied only by the twinkle in her eye. Mrs. Harris was rich, racy, colorful and of infinite good humor. ... she now owned the Hudson Theatre on 44th Street, a yacht and a stable of horses. She mentioned ... at our first meeting, I remember, that she had just turned down an offer of one million dollars for the Hudson Theatre [in 1929]."

"... Her inordinate liking for *The Beloved Bandit* was something I could not fathom then, nor can I understand it now, for she was theatrically shrewd and by no means a fool about plays in general—another proof, as though one were needed, that quite sensible people make fools of themselves about plays, with a relentless inevitability that fills half the theaters in New York each season with pure rubbish. In fact, her faith in *The Beloved Bandit* imbued us all with a foolish optimism and a ridiculous impatience to see the curtain rise as quickly as possible. ... Priestly Morrison, an actor of great charm and quite a good director in his own right, was engaged to stage the play, and I suspected almost at once that he thought *The Beloved Bandit* was absolute nonsense. In those days, however, directors did not pick and choose or wait around for a play they liked or respected. They took more or less what came their way, and since the theater was in a wildly flourishing state, it was common practice for a director to do as many as four or five plays in a season."

During the first stop out of town, in Rochester, Hart's *Beloved Bandit* was already in trouble. "But Mrs. Harris, a cigarette dangling from the corner of her mouth and a glass of beer in her hand, strode up and down the room as chirpy and cheerful as though the audience had acclaimed the play with sixteen curtain calls," Hart wrote in *Act One*. "She waved a hand to me as I came in and continued with what she had been saying."

"'I'll tell you something, boys,' she said, addressing me now as well as the others, 'the way it went tonight doesn't bother me one bit. Not a bit. You know why? First, this is Rochester—and what the hell does Rochester know about anything except Kodaks? Second, this is an audience play. I knew it when I read it and I still believe it. Give this play a chance with its own audience, boys, and you won't know you're watching the same play you saw tonight.'"

During the height of the booming Roaring Twenties, Mrs. Harris was lobbying Congress to repeal the so-called "Amusement Tax." She specifically said it helped reduce the number of "road shows" following a Broadway run. A decade later Mrs. Harris was fighting for her own survival, living off the kindness of friends and strangers.

They say in real estate that timing is everything. And Mrs. Harris, who was offered $1 million for the Hudson in 1929, saw it auctioned for $100,000 in 1932—or rather, did not see it. For years she refused to walk down 44th Street. It was sold in January 1932 to the Emigrant Industrial Savings Bank for the above mentioned sum of $100,000. It also had back taxes of $22,512. But before turning the page on the decade, *Clarence*, starring Alfred Lunt, opened at the Hudson Theatre in 1929 and became one of the theater's biggest hits. Lunt would soon marry an actress named Lynn Fontanne, and the greatest husband-and-wife acting team was born.

Here's a little of what my father had to say about them some half century ago:

> Alfred Lunt and Lynn Fontanne represent the most successful man-and-wife acting team in the history of the American theater. Lunt has been, certainly for me, the most fascinating actor on our native stage for the past thirty years. His technique in itself is irresistible—great strides about a living room, sudden changes in inflection and intonation, unsettling, hypnotic stares. Miss Fontanne, incredibly lovely to look upon from a down-front seat, retains her style and sparkle. Her laughter is as contagious as it always was; the zest which has always characterized her performances is undiminished.
>
> Lunt and Fontanne have been delighting audiences of Broadway, London's Shaftesbury Avenue and the American midlands ever since they first appeared together in *The Guardsman*. They had a romp in such plays as *Reunion in Vienna* and *Idiot's Delight*.
>
> I've had exciting sessions with Lunt and Fontanne in New York and London, in San Francisco and Chicago, in Lisbon and Atlanta and in Genesee Depot. It's when they're occupying their house of five chimneys in the tiny Wisconsin village, on Route 83, about forty-five minutes out of Milwaukee, it's when they're down on the

farm, as they call it, that they actually talk most about the theater, from which they're making a temporary escape.

Alfred, engaged in making his renowned Swedish hamburgers in the spacious and fabulously well-equipped kitchen at Genesee, will suddenly blurt out: "What a fine actor George Arliss was. Oh, I've met some wonderful, wonderful people in the theater. There was Olga Nethersole. One of my earliest memories in the theater was Miss Nethersole being carried up a flight of stairs in Clyde Fitch's play, *Sapho*, around 1901."

And then Lynn breaks in (they're always breaking in on each other but they never miss a word the other says): "Alfred, dear, you couldn't, you just couldn't have been going to the theater in 1901."

"My dear," says Alfred, his voice assuming the proportions of a pleasant roar, "I was very, very young, but I was going to the theater. ...Oh, I was with Margaret Anglin when I was starting. A very fine woman and a very fine actress."

Show business has probably always been a boom-or-bust industry. Even more so than Wall Street, daring men and women risk all on one throw of the dice. No doubt this is part of the appeal for those who have theater in their blood. I don't think Sophocles had to mortgage his house in Athens to mount *Oedipus Rex*, but I'll bet you he was pacing around madly at the back of the Odeon just before curtain time—even though it was long before the time of curtains in theaters. Such serendipity makes it all the more remarkable that such treasures at the Hudson have come down to us more or less intact. In many ways, the theaters themselves are the strongest rocks in an unusually rocky industry. Even if the producer, the playwright, the actor, and the financial supporters all go bust, someone is still going to buy the theater and try all over again. The theater building itself is the one thing the *Times* critic can't flatten. Not, I suppose, that from time to time over the years they haven't tried.

As a matter of fact, even when plays and musicals can no longer pay the theater building's rent, that doesn't necessarily mean the end. There are other fish to fry in show biz, and the Hudson would eventually try to earn its keep by playing host to those newfangled 20th-century curiosities: Radio and Television.

8

When Radio Was King

What a difference three years made. In 1929, riding high on successive George M. Cohan and other successful productions, Mrs. Harris was offered $1 million for the Hudson. In 1932, the Emigrant Industrial Savings Bank paid $100,000 for the property and there were those back taxes amounting to $22,512.

Producers Harry Askin and Hugh Ford reopened the Hudson in September 1932 in the depths of the Great Depression in the heartfelt belief they would return it to the fold of legitimate Broadway playhouses, once again resuming production. In an article appearing in the September 14, 1932, edition of *The New York Sun*, a paper my father wrote his "Broadway After Dark" column for, the producers announced that their theater ticket prices would start at the somewhat astounding sum of 50 cents and range up to $2.50.

"At that time when taxes, interest, and insurance were extremely high for the theater, lower prices were only justified by the mere hopes of increasing patronage," the Landmarks Commission wrote in its assessment of the Hudson. "Reducing the stagehand's wages in order to lower operating costs was even considered in order not to increase prices. There were many expenses in the theater and it was difficult for management not to charge a higher price.

"Mr. Askin pointed out that of all of the theaters in New York which have passed through financial difficulty, the Hudson was the first to be given a new chance as a Broadway theater again. Emigrant Bank's source of money enabled the theater to be refurbished. It was very

Drawing of my father, drama critic of the old New York Sun, which accompanied his "Broadway After Dark" column appearing in 1926.

common to see theaters that were on the financial rocks get run down. More than $300,000 was spent on refurbishing it.

"Therein Mr. Askin gave the first sign that theaters were working their way out of the hands of real estate interests and back into the hands of showmen. He said that theaters were too prosperous for their own good in the years immediately following the war. Shows were produced in such great numbers that the theater managers could demand guarantees from the producers up to as much as $5,000 a week. Consequently, the theater became a real estate proposition. There were about seventy legitimate playhouses at that time. However, once business returned to normal levels, there would only be use for about forty theaters."

On February 3, 1934, a new "Radio Theatre" opened at the Hudson, giving the theater new life through the Great Depression. The opening of the Columbia Broadcasting System's CBS Playhouse gave the public the opportunity to see their favorite radio stars live and up close. The opening night capacity crowd [was] treated to the antics of critic and radio personality Alexander Woollcott and actress Ruth Etting. It was the first radio broadcast with a live studio audience. Commentator Edwin Hill made opening remarks followed by performances by Nino Martini, a tenor; Albert Spalding, violinist; Alexander Woollcott and comedian George Jessel.

For the man immortalized as the king of radio in Kaufman and Hart's *The Man Who Came to Dinner*, Alexander Woollcott's first time on radio practically scared him to death. "His tongue clacked,"

Samuel Hopkins Adams says in *A. Woollcott*, his biography of the drama critic turned radio star. "He lost his sense of timing. His words, as he painfully read, were being distorted by that mysterious and malevolent little contraption (radio mike) into something quite alien to himself." He gradually became more adept in what was a new and challenging medium for him, so much so that he could be classified as one of radio's brightest all-talking stars of the 1930's. The late Bennett Cerf would write in his book *Try and Stop Me* that, as a reviewer of books on the radio, "Woollcott's enthusiasms could make a book a best-seller."

Nevertheless, one aspect of radio showmanship drove Woollcott, the veteran theater reviewer, to distraction. This was the so-called "public" radios, as they were labeled at the Hudson, to which audiences attended and clapped or laughed on cue. Woollcott was so exasperated with this practice that he once urged his fellow radio guests to cry out "lousy" when they were asked to applaud. However, reason and his very ample weekly paycheck prevailed.

In the middle of the CBS Radio Playhouse show, an announcer broke in to present songs by Bing Crosby, music by Guy Lombardo and his Orchestra and a comedy sketch by Burns and Allen. The 1,200-member audience at the former Hudson listened to this "West Coast" interlude which was broadcast from a California studio and fed into the theater over the public address system.

"The opening performance was to be followed by other series of broadcasts devoted to special purposes before invited audiences as well," the New York City Landmarks Preservation Commission wrote in their history of the Hudson. It continued:

> There were plans to do some of the broadcasting for Columbia's School of the Air before educators who would have an opportunity to be more informed about what was happening in educational broadcasting. The Radio Playhouse would also be used to extend Columbia's involvement in musical education. Selected audiences of music students and educators would be invited to hear special broadcasts and lectures by Columbia's notable conductors.
>
> Development of the technique of dramatic productions was also

another purpose to which the Playhouse stage studio would be utilized. CBS stated that more attention was being paid in 1934 than ever before to dramatic productions.

Consequently, CBS engineers equipped the theater with the very latest type of broadcasting equipment, including acoustical arrangements which were expected to make the stage one of the most distinguished studios in the world. The theater was adapted for broadcasting and equipped with the latest radio devices as well. A unique feature of the studio theater was the glass-enclosed control room in one of the boxes, so that audience members could view the production as enacted on the stage. All of these features helped make the theater, then and now, one of the most technically advanced theaters on Broadway.

In February of 1937, the CBS Radio Playhouse was changed back to its original name, the Hudson Theatre. CBS returned the theater back to its original fold. Once a tenant was found, the new managers, Sam H. Grisman and Jack Kirkland, planned to return the Hudson to a legitimate playhouse again.

The Hudson wasn't the first radio studio in Times Square. The roof of the New Amsterdam Theatre was used as a studio as well starting in 1930. The New Amsterdam Roof first opened in 1904, living through a series of theater-related ventures before 1930; it had opened in 1915 as the Danse de Follies, presenting Florenz Ziegfeld's "Midnight Frolics."

After the advent of radio at the Hudson, Mrs. Harris was profiled in 1936 by the New York *World-Telegram*. It's so telling, I give it to you in its entirety. The headline alone speaks volumes: "Mrs. Harris, Happy in WPA Stage Job, Again Can Look Old Theater in the Eye."

>Mrs. Harris, widow of the theatrical producer who went down in the *Titanic* twenty-four years ago this April, and who ran her husband's business for fifteen years, lost all her money in a producing venture which closed the theater four years ago.
>
>More, she lost heart. And though she tried to carry on, writing an occasional article, a bit of verse, selling cocktail trays of her

own design and make, it was not until a few weeks ago that she held a weekly pay check in her hand again—a WPA check—for her work in conjunction with the Federal Theatre.

"And you don't know how thrilled I was," she said. "To be independent again. That's what it meant. I had been forced into a parasitical existence, living off my sister and her husband. The check that comes every Wednesday now is a godsend. It looks as big as all outdoors to me."

Three One-Act Plays

Sunday night, the first of Mrs. Harris' production efforts as a WPA worker will be presented. It's a showing of three one-act plays, Susan Glaspell's "Close the Book," "The Beggar and the King" and a dramatization of Ernest Hemingway's short story, "The Killers," which she arranged herself.

There's one street in New York which Mrs. Henry B. Harris has not set foot on since 1932. That's the block in 44th St. between Sixth Ave. and Broadway, which houses the building that was once...the Harris, then the Hudson Theatre.

The performance will be given by the Rand players, in the Rand School Playhouse, 7 E. 15th St.

Mrs. Harris is the only WPA worker in this group of young experimental players, but the Federal Theatre project is giving her her crew, her scenery, her lighting equipment—"everything we need," she said jubilantly.

"Perhaps I'll be able to walk down 44th St. again, now," she said. "I'll never forget the night I knew it was all over, that I'd failed. I came out of the theater, disconsolate. I walked up the street and I glanced back over my shoulder. There, in the marquee, still lighted—for I hadn't waited for the finish—I read what seemed to be my doom, 'Never No More,' the name of the play I had just quit."

But after the nervous breakdown in which her friends rallied round, her spirit came back. She made a few dollars here and there. And she began working with amateurs, experimental players, producing this play and that.

WINS HIGH PRAISE

One, *Maedchen in Uniform*, won high praise from critics, one calling the amateur performance more finished, the direction more sensitive, than the professional presentation on Broadway.

"But while I loved it, while it was all I really knew how to do, I couldn't keep it up," she said. "We were working on a co-operative basis, and I sometimes didn't even get carfare out.

"However, a little while after I left, a group of twelve girls called on me. So I started all over again. I produced *The Question Before the House* with the Rand School players. A few days before opening I heard that Hallie Flanagan, director of the Federal Theatre project, had directed it at Vasser. I wired her asking her if she could come. She replied with a charming wire, but she was en route to Washington.

"Then next thing I knew I was persuaded to make my application to WPA, and they came to my assistance, with a salary and all the technical assistance I need. And somehow I feel the tide has turned and everything's going to be all right."

During the 1930's Broadway reeled under the effects of the Great Depression which dramatically slashed the number of yearly productions from their late-1920's high of over 275. The Hudson itself went from a million dollar asset to a liability as the new decade dawned. As radio became the Hudson's salvation, vaudeville, which had flourished at the nearby Palace Theatre, went the way of the Times Square lobster palace. The outstanding plays of the decade included Vicki Baum's *Grand Hotel* (made into a movie with John Barrymore, Greta Garbo and a young and very appealing Joan Crawford) and Eugene O'Neill's *Mourning Becomes Electra*. There were also, in this decade, outstanding performances by the likes of Katharine Hepburn in *The Philadelphia Story* and Leslie Howard in *The Petrified Forest*. Howard would re-create his lead role in the film of the same name which most famously brought immediate stardom to one Humphrey Bogart who played gangster Duke Mantee on Broadway and in the movie—the latter at the insistence of Howard who said he wouldn't do the movie unless Bogart did it as well.

But by the turn of the decade, as Poland reeled under the Nazis, the theater, the legitimate Broadway theater, returned once again to the Hudson as radio moved into new studios and the demand for playhouses grew. Opening in November 1940 a play called *Fledgling,* based on a book called *Follow the Furies* by Eleanor Carroll Chilton, "not only holds the attention (of the audience) but in general merits it," John Mason Brown said in his review of the play in the *New York Post.* About a mercy killing and a suicide, it "is a courageous play," Brown continued, "adult in its dilemmas and in much of its thinking. In this war year, so undistinguished in its dramatic output, when most managers have surrendered to the fallacy that comedy, good or bad, but comedy alone would be acceptable, it proudly goes on its way, daring to raise issues not ordinarily raised in the theater."

So, once again, despite the war raging in Europe, despite radio's hold on the Hudson in particular and the American public in general, drama, American drama, was king in the house that Henry built. It would indeed take lighter turns with productions of *Arsenic and Old Lace* and *State of the Union* before getting back to drama again with *The Detective Story* toward the close of the decade.

The Hudson, meanwhile, was taking on a little of the quality of the Unsinkable Molly Brown. Molly famously did not go down with the *Titanic*. The theater's owner and founding father Henry Harris had succumbed to the waves, but the theater itself seemingly defied the crushing effects of several attempts to swamp it over the course of many decades. Adapting to the new medium of radio was only one of its deft financial moves. Nor was the theater itself the only canny survivor in the building. There was a man and his family who somehow came to live in the Hudson Theatre who showed survival instincts that might have impressed even the great Molly Brown herself.

9

The Strange Case of Mr. Breen

Enter the strange case of Wilva and Robert Breen who occupied the "apartment" above the marquee of the Hudson from 1942 to the late 1990's. Mr. Breen and his family make for the kind of story that seemingly could only happen in The Theater. His story in many ways is more dramatic than anything that had been formally presented on the Hudson's stage for many a year.

Breen, who was executive director of the American National Theatre & Academy (ANTA) and a legitimate producer of shows and ballet, actually lived at the theater in the 2500-square-foot duplex apartment space through thirteen owners of the theater. At one time, Breen lived in the third- and fourth-floor duplex with his wife and seven other people including a cousin and a business associate. I venture to say that never before in the history of show business has such an odd array of people occupied so unusual a space.

In one telling episode during that remarkable period, Mr. Breen addressed himself and his interests to the august representative of the last in the string of these otherwise formidable new landlords. At least an entity of the magnitude of U.S. Steel would appear formidable to anyone other than Mr. Breen.

WILVA & ROBERT BBREEN
139 WEST 44TH STREET
NEW YORK, NEW YORK 10036

June 12, 1979

Irvin T. Pollack,
Esq. 555 Fifth Avenue
New York, New York 10017
      Re: 139 West 44

Dear Mr. Pollack:
Re your 6 June letter:
 Your client, upon inspection of our place recently, must certainly have been aware that we had absolutely NO intention whatsoever of moving out—what with the repairs and re-decoration, etc. going forward, plus our restoration of the Roof, and re-caulking of the roof-hatch. We have, incidentally, installed three new roofs since our occupancy.
 Mr. Schuck, of the Dwyer Agency, and those concerned at U.S. STEEL certainly knew first-hand that we had no "moving" plans—nor do we have right now.
 Your client is the ninth (9th) purchaser of the Hudson since our occupancy—which commenced in November 1942—while I was still in the U.S. Air Force. Mrs. Henry B. Harris, widow of the builder of the Hudson, was instrumental in making this place headquarters for our work.
 Since that time, all Mrs. Breen's and my professional lives have been devoted to non-profit organizations—to which I devoted full service—never accepting any salary.
 We are not just "living" at 139 West 44. We constantly receive scholars and researchers from Europe and the USA, to inspect our files with respect to their work.
 We have here the early files of the AMERICAN NATIONAL THEATRE & ACADEMY (Chartered by Congress)—and files re the United States' very first cultural exchanges with Russia, Poland, Czechoslovakia, and Latin America—all of which Mrs. Breen and I arranged.
 From 1944 to 1950, I was the Executive Director of the American National Theatre & Academy, serving without salary. Mrs. Breen was the Assistant.
 In 1950 we made all arrangements, sending the AMERICAN BALLET THEATER Company on tour through Europe—which marked

the very first, and, history-making, visit of an American ballet company to Europe.

Also history-making was the four-year international tour (1952-56) of PORGY AND BESS, which Mrs. Breen produced and I directed for EVERYMAN OPERA (also a non-profit entity). I accepted no salary nor Director's percentage. (See Tour-List enclosed.)

There have been nine (9) owners of the Hudson Theatre since our occupancy. One of these owners, in an apparent effort to induce us to leave 139, informed us they were definitely planning demolition of the Hudson, and, that they already had a demolition-permit from the City.

However, our friends at *The New York Times* ascertained within a half-hour that this was not true, nor was it likely that the City would ever issue a permit to demolish the Hudson—which is the oldest theater in the Broadway district.

Very truly yours,
Robert Breen

Enclosures: Programs, etc.
                      The rent checks for May and June
                      which you returned to us.

Breen himself, a producer, as articulate as he was astute, avoided eviction by shifting between graciousness and righteous indignation.

"We have worked hard, sacrificed too much, and started too important a movement in the theater to casually relinquish the place after just a few new months of civilian life," Breen wrote Howard Lindsay and Russel Crouse who owned the theater in February 1946. "Without meaning to flap the flag in your faces, there are 9 veterans (plus others) cooperatively sharing the place, and devoting their time to laying groundwork for the National Theater Foundation, which Bob Porterfield and I set forth and which has just been adopted by the American National Theatre & Academy, Inc. as its mode of operation. Bob and the rest of us have really pushed hard toward this end. Bob has his Barter Theatre N. Y. headquarters here also. Over and above,

National Theatre Foundation

Establishment of a Theatre, national in scope, yet individual in initiative, by means of a National Theatre Foundation which will sponsor and aid various types of theatre activity to fit the diverse needs of the country.

The majority of National Theatre plans promulgated within the last 50 years have been patterned after European types. There are many good individual theatre plans, any one of which might be termed by its originators as a "National Theatre," but no *one* of which (no matter how worthwhile individually) could alone serve the theatrical needs of the entire country. Our traditional spirit of individual enterprise makes possible the individual working out of forms of theatre best suited to each community. Any plan to implement the Theatre in really serving the country must be as flexible and as versatile as America itself.

Therefore, in 1946, The American National Theatre and Academy (after eleven years of inactivity since receiving its Congressional Charter in 1935) adopted as its basic principle of operation the NATIONAL THEATRE FOUNDATION plan.

The NATIONAL THEATRE FOUNDATION is simple and broad—an all-embracing National Theatre plan elastic enough to facilitate the developement of all existing projects for more and better Theatre, and to materialize future plans and projects as they arise from the needs of the times. Under ANTA it is an official instrument through which all interests and factions in the Theatre can channel energies for a common cause, and for materialization of their own individual projects. The NATIONAL THEATRE FOUNDATION is a theatre plan fitted to the needs of America. It can be a practical framework for the creation of abundant theatre in the United States.

The ANTA NATIONAL THEATRE FOUNDATION plan is the first National Theatre concept to catch the interest of the country at large. It has achieved this because the plan itself is not committed to any *single* type of theatre project or idea. ANTA is the property of the people of the Theatre who use it—and it will grow and change as they make it grow and change. The national objective is long-range and cannot be accomplished by magic or wishing or hoping. The success of any plan depends on the integrity and willingness to serve on the part of those involved, and especially on a long campaign of hard and unremitting work.

The NATIONAL THEATRE FOUNDATION entails the pooling of ideas, resources, knowledge, in the sponsorship, stimulation and support of all phases of good Theatre for the country as a whole. In one sense it will be a fund which will make loans, grants, guarantees against loss, for the purpose of theatre activity on the basis of quality and standard of material and projects submitted, and on the demonstrated need of the community or territory concerned.

Some individuals are inclined to dub the FOUNDATION idea as "vague" and "visionary" and "lacking in specifics." Everyone here has greatly envied England and its Arts Council of Great Britain, which operates according to a very simple central theme—the following *statement of purposes*:

"The defined purpose of the Council is to maintain the highest standard in the arts. The Council hopes to enlist in this policy the cooperation of theatre companies which have before them the same ideals of service to the community; which are anxious to spread the knowledge and appreciation of all that is best in the theatre, and thus to bring into being permanent educated audiences all over the country."

The Arts Council, as Lord Keynes told ANTA in 1946, has no set of complex rules and regulations. It cues its action to the above stated principle and deals with each submitted theatre project on its own terms, and there is nothing at all "vague" about the operation of it. The major difference between the Arts Council and ANTA is that the Arts Council enjoys a yearly financial grant from the British Treasury.

The NATIONAL THEATRE FOUNDATION idea, which forms the basis of both organizations, was promulgated here in the United States in 1940, but got lost in the shuffle prior to our entering the war. Subsequently, England utilized the very same principle in its CEMA (Council for the Encouragement of Music and The Arts). The first sizable funds to support CEMA came through an American, Edward S. Harkness, who contributed to the Pilgrims' Trust. In 1942, the British Treasury granted funds to CEMA. In 1946, CEMA was awarded a Royal Charter and was renamed The Arts Council of Great Britain.

We hear speeches every day prefaced by "*when* we have a National Theatre" or "*if* we had a National Theatre." We already *have* a National Theatre recognized by our Government and the world, which can expand Theatre in every direction because it is designed for that purpose. ANTA has not waited for funds in order to operate on a FOUNDATION plan; since its inception, ANTA has functioned on a foundation of services given freely and effectively for the advancement of the American Theatre.

Robert Breen

Robert Breen, whose family lived in the apartment above the Hudson Theatre for many years, helped establish the National Theatre Foundation which he hoped would become an American version of Great Britain's National Theatre. There have many successful not-for-profit theaters in America, including the Lincoln Center Theater and the New York Public Theatre but, alas, a national theater, funded by taxpayer dollars, has yet to blossom fully despite sporatic attempts like the National Theatre Foundation we have a Veterans' Counseling Service which is sponsored by the National Theater Conference.

"As things stand, we shall be at 139 for quite some time after the expiration of the present lease, despite your notice of termination. It would be uncomfortable indeed knowing that we were staying on only because the government has made protective provisions for such cases.

"So, since we have a long and increasingly important job ahead of us, and since it certainly doesn't take a CPA to know that we need the space more than you do, give this matter the grace of a second thought and sign at least a five (5) year lease with us."

Breen's lease didn't actually expire until September 20, 1946, but he was asked to leave so that "extensive repairs" could be made in his apartment.

Breen once said (in 1979) that, "139 is, and never has been, just a 'residence' for us.

"Prior to the end of the War, Wilva and I and others had been promulgating the idea of creation of a National Foundation for the Arts. Soon after I was discharged from the Air Force, we started (at 139) what turned out to be an historic movement.

"The American National Theatre & Academy (Chartered by Congress) appointed Wilva and myself as the Executive Directors—to launch the nation-wide campaign for support. (We did not take salaries.) All this work for the next 7-8 years emanated from 139—with a big regular staff of volunteers.

"In those days—climbing our steps daily along with the volunteer staff—were Mrs. Roosevelt, Helen Hayes (who was President of ANTA), John Garfield, Charles Laughton, Ethel Barrymore, Judith Anderson ... and hosts of others.

"As we all know, the country now has the National Endowment for the Arts, and other governmental support for the Arts. Also, we launched, with the Department of State, the first European tour of an American ballet company (the American Ballet Theatre)—and the four-year European and Latin American tour of Gershwin's PORGY AND BESS—which Mrs. Breen and I produced and I directed. This was also a non-profit-foundation-project."

Breen at one time tried to get the New York Shakespeare Festival to move to the Hudson.

>Mr. Joseph Papp
>New York Shakespeare Festival
>Public Theatre
>425 Lafayette
>New York, New York 10003
>
>Dear Joseph Papp:
>Please note the enclosed proposal to the President of U.S. Steel re: the Hudson Theatre—and you.
>   Am wondering whether you are aware that U.S. Steel expended $150,000 redecorating the interior of the Hudson after they expelled the porno-film operation.
>   YOU are the only person in charge of the Hudson—if U.S. Steel decides to donate it.
>
>   Hearty Cheers to you,
>   and your grand work!
>   <initialed>
>   Wilva and Robert Breen
>
>   P.S. And, please forgive the use of "American" rather than "New York" in one instance in the letter to Steel.

Breen was such a master of survival that, had he put as much effort into producing plays as he did staying put above the Hudson, he might have given the late David Merrick a good run for his money in the department of producing credits. In the process of staying put Breen angered a succession of owners. Ron Delsener blamed him for cutting into his possible revenues by not permitting him to use the apartment for VIP ticket holders. The Landmarks Commission, researching the history of the theater, offered this account of Breen's tenancy:

    It was Irene Harris who informed Robert Breen, a stage and

screen producer, about the vacant a/partme7nts over the Hudson Theatre. She was aware that the Shuberts, who were leasing the theater at the time, were looking for a tenant. The Shuberts demanded that the Breens submit a letter from their doctor stating that they were in good health because the only access to the apartment was four steep flights of stairs.

Mr. Breen rented nine rooms, divided between the third and fourth floors. He lived there with his wife, Wilva; twin stepsons, Paul and William Martin; Paul's wife, Ethel Ayler, a principal in the impending musical, *Kwamina*; Mrs. Breen's mother, Florence Davis; Ed Martin, a cousin, and Robert Dustin, a business associate.

Mr. Breen made his own repairs and supplied his own janitorial service. He obtained heat and hot water only when the theater was occupied. Otherwise, he had to rely on electric heaters and fireplaces.

In an interview, Wilva Breen recalled the day Robert left her in charge of the apartment. "Robert took the place one day then went off to war and left me in it," she laughed.

It is not unusual for there to be apartments above the Hudson Theatre. Prior to WWI, almost all theaters were built with suites of offices or bedrooms on the upper floors. At that time, being involved in the theater was considered a meaningless job, therefore, people involved in that industry could not live or work anywhere else. But Mrs. Breen is the last person in the city who still lives in one of the old theaters. The other tenants died or moved away long ago, and the space was never rented out again. Mrs. Breen had to face many persistent and nagging owners in order to remain in her apartment. All thirteen of the landlords managing the Hudson have tried to evict her family without success.

Breen himself even had the tenacity and audacity to write this time not to the attorney but to the president of United States Steel:

139 WEST 44TH—NEW YORK 10036—PL 7 5283
ROBERT BREEN   WILVA DAVIS

January 18, 1979

Mr. David M. Roderick, President
United States Steel
767 Fifth Avenue
New York, N.Y. 10022

Dear Mr. Roderick: Re: the HUDSON Theater

In certain circles, we have, to hearty cheers, broached the following idea:

That U.S. STEEL and the CARNEGIE PENSION FUND very seriously consider donation of the Hudson Theater to:

> The KENNEDY CENTER for the PERFORMING ARTS
> in Washington, D.C.
> and
> The NEW YORK SHAKESPEARE FESTIVAL
> in New York City

Both organizations are Foundation-funded.

The Tax-branch of your legal staff could quickly ascertain the considerable donation-benefits on the part of U.S. Steel—as opposed to the possible sale of the theater for $800,000.

In addition, U.S. Steel, which apparently has no great ostensible record of financially aiding the Arts—as have so many other large corporations—would be forever remembered locally and nationally.

The Hudson Theater would be utilized mainly for New York presentation of promising productions incoming from the extensive list of non-profit, foundation-funded theater organizations through-out the nation. There are about seventy (70) such institutions.

Also, right here in New York City, there are about eighty (80) or so "OFF BROADWAY" and "OFF-OFF-BROADWAY" theaters. These organizations are nonprofit, and, of course, mainly foundation-funded.

As is well-known, some of the really interesting plays are launched by these theater-organizations, and there is need for a theater (such as the Hudson) to which the most promising of these productions can be transferred to the "Broadway" area.

In addition, interesting foreign theater companies, dance and musical groups could appear at the Hudson.

****

Incidentally, immediately after your organization "cleared" the Hudson of that dreadful "porno"-film operation, I spoke to the Hudson Manager about the musical, CHORUS LINE, which was then aborning under the aegis of the New York Shakespeare Festival down-town. I strongly urged this manager-chap to immediately contact Mr. Joseph Papp, producer of the piece. Sorry to relate, the Hudson manager gave me rather short shrift, negating the idea.

As we all know now, CHORUS LINE did move uptown and is still running on 44th Street, at the Shubert Theater, doing capacity income.

****

Be certain, dear sir, donation of the Hudson would engender lasting national and local appreciation and kudos for U.S. Steel.

All good wishes
<signature>
Robert Breen

In a small twist of fate, the Hudson and *A Chorus Line* were destined to meet again in the future. The cast and crew from a revival of the Pulitzer Prize- and Tony Award-winning musical *A Chorus Line* made their first public appearance at the historic Hudson Theatre in Times Square on April 26, 2006. The record-breaking musical that wowed Broadway in the 1970's and '80's was slated to make its big return to Broadway in the fall of that year, at the Gerald Schoenfeld Theatre, directed by its original Tony Award winning co-choreographer, Bob Avian.

The original *A Chorus Line* had opened at the New York Shakespeare Festival's Newman Theatre on May 21, 1975, and transferred to Broadway's Shubert Theatre on July 25th, although the official Broadway opening night there wasn't until October 19th. The funny, heart-tugging musical about, you guessed it, a Broadway chorus line's struggling members, won the Pulitzer Prize for Drama, nine Tony Awards including Best Musical, Score and Book, and the New York Drama Critics Circle Award. It ran for nearly 15 years, closing on April 28, 1990, after 6,137 performances. *A Chorus Line* remains one of the longest-running American musicals in Broadway history and no doubt will remain so for a very long time.

Breen's tenacity also probably saved the theater from the wrecking ball. Nine years after Breen moved in, after the National Broadcasting Company sold the theater to Samuel Lehren, a garage builder and operator, Breen refused to move even though he was told by an NBC representative the company "would be ready to compensate you on a very fair basis." Replying to this Breen stated, "Judging from your letter, it appears that NBC has now decided not to go through with the projected sale of the Hudson Theater building, which involved ultimate demolition of the structure for the purpose of erecting a garage. Would you please outline to me in detail—in writing—exactly what your company has in mind with reference to my tenancy?"

In writing to his wife, Wilva, Breen told of a letter he wrote to playwrights and producers, Lindsay and Crouse, who also owned the theater for a while. "My letter is a little stiffer than planned, but I think is OK. I told them we'd be here ANYWAY, so might as well sign lease," he wrote. Breen, as shown earlier in this chapter, also wrote the late Joseph Papp of the New York Shakespeare Festival to see if he was willing to assume operation of the theater. Belatedly, although it had not been a porno house since 1973, Kitty Carlisle Hart, playwright Moss Hart's widow, wrote to Breen in 1979 congratulating him for helping turn it back into a legitimate theater. Mrs. Hart's letter follows:

NYSCA
NEW YORK STATE COUNCIL ON THE ARTS
80 CENTRE STREET
NEW YORK. N.Y. 10013
212 488-5222

January 30, 1979
Mr. Robert Breen
139 West 44th Street
New York, New York 10036

Dear Robert Breen:
Thanks you so much for your kind note.
Our Off-Off Broadway theaters are indeed a boon to the theater community in New York. Thank heavens the Hudson is no longer a porno house and that (we hope!) through your efforts it will now begin to house, once again, legitimate theatrical activity.

>Best, as ever
>\<signature\>
>Kitty Carlisle Hart
>Chairman
>mg

It seems almost insane now that anyone could seriously have considered tearing down one of New York's oldest and most celebrated playhouses to put up a parking garage. That would be like Paris tearing down the Eiffel Tower to build a supermarket. At no time in America's history has "legitimate" theater been a natural money-making proposition, certainly not when compared to the fortunes of U.S. Steel or NBC. What has kept theater, and its great institutions like the Hudson, alive is the dedicated theater person. Not all have been as embattled as Mr. and Mrs. Breen, but it is their breed to whom we owe the survival of much our national theater culture.

Another great dedicated New York theater person was Kitty Carlisle Hart herself. Alas, she died during the writing of this book and was instantly mourned by the whole city, but especially the theater people. At eight p.m. the night she died, Broadway lights dimmed in tribute.

"She died at her New York apartment," close friend, singer Kathleen Landis told Reuters. "Kitty came into the Café Pierre a few weeks ago and she didn't look herself." Kathleen Landis has sung at the Café Pierre in New York's Hotel Pierre for twenty years. She knows perhaps better than anyone the exalted place her good friend Kitty Hart held for so long in New York society. "Even if the Mayor of New York, Michael Bloomberg, had a wife," Ms. Landis explained, "Kitty would still be the first lady of New York. Everyone thought of Kitty as that."

Ms. Hart, who would have been 97 on September 3, 2007, was probably best known for having been a regular on the phenomenal hit TV show *To Tell the Truth*. Hart was born in New Orleans, the daughter of a doctor, and educated in some of the best schools in Europe before embarking on a life-long career on stage and in concert halls, radio and television. Her most famous early movie role was in the Marx Brothers' movie classic *A Night at the Opera* in 1934. Broadway theater owner Stewart F. Lane, who is currently co-producer of the hit musical *Legally Blond*, remembers Hart losing her balance at a gala for the Broadway Theatre Museum at the Hudson Theatre last fall. "But before anyone could help her she was sitting down and had her dinner! She was phenomenal as a human being and, more than anyone else I can think of, represented the history of entertainment in the 20th century."

At least by association it can be argued that interest in starting a national theater in this country really gained some momentum at the Hudson through Breen, even though it remains an idea whose time has still to come to any real fruition.

Chartered by Congress in 1935, the American National Theatre and Academy created the National Theatre Foundation in 1946. A program for a gala commemorating the establishment of the National Theatre Foundation stressed the ideals of the Foundation. "The pooling of ideas, resources, knowledge, in the sponsorship, stimulation and support of all phases of good theater for the country as a whole," Breen wrote in the program. "We hear speeches every day prefaced by 'when we have a national theater...' We already have a national theater recognized by our own government and the world, and we can expand Theatre in every direction because it is designed for that purpose."

It's probably safe to say that the last time any government seriously imagined founding a truly "national" theater was during the Thirties and Forties. Not since FDR has any congress or president expressed serious interest in funding the arts. Furthermore, the advent of television, and public television in particular, has diverted a lot of what federal tax dollars are available for such enterprises—perhaps rightly so, since only television can truly reach a "national" audience.

The closest America has come in recent years to having a "national" theater, something along the lines of the Old Vic in London or the Comédie-Française in Paris, is the Kennedy Center for the Performing Arts in Washington, D.C. Though it does indeed celebrate American talent, it doesn't present definitive productions of American-written plays, such as those of Tennessee Williams or Eugene O'Neill, in the glorious way Shakespeare is "officially" immortalized in England or Molière in France. But at least Robert Breen gave creation of an American national theater a good, long try.

All good things must come to an end, however, and the long saga of the Breen clan's occupation of the Hudson's lone apartment finally came to a close not that many years ago, when Breen's elderly widow finally vacated the premises. "She lived right through into the late 1990's," one former Broadway Millennium Hotel executive told me. "The apartment above the theater had no elevator, and in Mrs. Breen's son's mind at least, the stairs had become too much for her to climb. He took her to live closer to his home." This means that a member of the Breen family lived in the Hudson Theatre from 1942 until just before the turn of the 21st century, or more than half a century.

10

Comedy and Drama Return to the Hudson

*A*rsenic and Old Lace, a hit at the Hudson Theatre in 1943, opened originally at the Fulton Theatre on January 10, 1941, to rave reviews. Boris Karloff, who repeated his role in the movie version with Cary Grant, was the original Jonathan Brewster. "Mr. Karloff has charge of most of the horror and he is over-poweringly sinister in a performance that would, I should think, scare the other actors out of their make-up," wrote critic John Anderson in his review in the *New York Journal-American*. "Josephine Hull is wonderful as a ducky little murderess ..."

In 1945 Howard Lindsay and Russel Crouse's political play, *State of the Union*, was awarded the Pulitzer Prize for best original play of the 1945-46 season. It opened on November 14, 1945, and ran all through 1946 and well into 1947 as the country moved from a war-time to a peace economy and Broadway become reinvigorated. It co-starred Myron McCormick, Minor Watson, and Kay Johnson. It opened just after *The Hasty Heart* by John Patrick closed after 204 performances. (Russel Crouse, incidentally, had collaborated with my father without official credit in his Broadway play *Gentlemen of the Press* seventeen years earlier.)

"With *State of the Union* the current state of the theater becomes enriched for Howard Lindsay and Russel Crouse; the scenarists of *Life With Father* have made an adult, witty play about politics," wrote John

Comedy and Drama Return to the Hudson ~ 97

"Arsenic and Old Lace," about two maiden aunts who poison their borders, became such a hit at the Fulton Theatre it moved to the Hudson. Boris Karloff, who played the monster in the "Frankenstein" movies, was in the cast on stage. He was replaced by Raymond Massey in the film version, released in 1944. PHOTO BY LINCOLN CENTER LIBRARY FOR THE PERFORMING ARTS

Chapman in the *New York Daily News*. "This *State of the Union* is the smash hit for which the theatrical season has been waiting," wrote Robert Garland in the *Journal-American*. The play, starring film actor Ralph Bellamy as an airplane manufacturer who runs for president, "provides one of the few worthwhile evenings that has come from the

New York theater this season," wrote Ward Morehouse in his review in *The New York Sun*. These and other critics were unanimous in their belief the play was as meaningful as it was entertaining and vice versa. But at the heart it was not about a politician per se but an idealist: liberal and independent, certainly, but an idealist nevertheless who lets his conscience guide him in the end.

State of the Union had been picked by the Columbia University Pulitzer committee on the first ballot as the best American play of 1945-1946. The play was actually suggested in a roundabout fashion by Helen Hayes, one of the greatest actresses of the American theater of the 20th century. Miss Hayes married ex-newspaperman and playwright Charles MacArthur (co-author of the megahit *The Front Page*). But she had a huge crush on Alfred Lunt, her co-star in *Clarence* at the Hudson Theatre a quarter century earlier. When Lunt was visited backstage night after night by Lynn Fontanne, his soon-to-be-wife, Hayes and other female *Clarence* company members were alternately green with envy and red with jealousy.

The authors of *Life with Father* had a comedy in mind for Miss Hayes and conferences were being held but, Burns Mantle wrote in the 1945-46 edition of *Best Plays*, "Then Miss Hayes decided that what she needed more than a new play was a year's rest from constant devotion to the theater. So she went back to her Nyack (New York) estate and the playwrights returned to their search for a proper subject."

Lindsay and Crouse had agreed there might be a good comedy with a touch of political significance somewhere in the colorful adventures of the late Wendell Wilkie. His nomination and campaign for the presidency in 1940 had furnished excitement enough for a dozen plays. But the conviction that their play should not in any sense be a Wilkie play was definitely fixed in the minds of both authors. To combine politics and romance in the same comedy is a good trick if you can do it. As it turned out *State of the Union* became a very human domestic comedy with serious dramatic overtones.

The following two years, 1947 and 1948, saw no hits but some big names. In 1948, *Jenny Kissed Me* by Jean Kerr, who would later gain fame for *Please Don't Eat the Daisies* and other writings, starred Leo G. Carroll and Ann Baxter. Then in 1949 the Hudson had a solid hit with *Detective Story* by Sidney Kingsley, also produced by Lindsay and Crouse. It starred Lee Grant, Lou Gilbert, Patrick McVey, Earl Sydnor, Maureen Stapleton, Meg Mundy, Alexander Scourby, Joseph Wiseman, John Boyd, Les Tremayne, Edward Binns, Warren Stevens, Jean Adair and James Westerfield and ran for 581 performances.

Horace McMahon, who years later starred in the TV series of *Detective Story*, liked to frequent the Lambs Club across the street from the Hudson, when I was living there in the early 1970's. The club, which lost the Stanford White clubhouse across from the theater in the 1970's, currently occupies the fifth floor of the Women's National Republican Club at 3 West 51st Street.

In 1946 Eugene O'Neill and his wife Carlotta were on tour with *The Iceman Cometh*. They were staying at the Wentworth Hotel near the Hudson when a press conference was arranged for him. He surprised reporters with an attack on what he felt was the country's spiritual bankruptcy. O'Neill, of course, didn't live to see how far Times Square went downhill two decades later nor how much it would then improve in the late 1990's. "I am going on the theory that the United States, instead of being the most successful country in the world, is the greatest failure ... because it was given everything, more than any other country. ... We are the greatest example of, 'For what shall it profit man if he shall gain the whole world, and lose his own soul?'"

My father knew O'Neill personally and was even invited to his estate in France called Le Plessis. That was in 1930 and O'Neill wrote, in minute handwriting, in a letter sent to my father at London's Savoy Hotel:

LE PLESSIS
SAINT-ANTOINE DU ROCHER
(INDRE-ET-LOIRE)

March 29th, 1930

Dear Ward Morehouse:

Sure thing! I'll be glad to see you. Arrange to come down and stay over night with us. There's a good train from Paris to Tours around two or two-thirty p.m. that gets in Tours around six. Wire me a couple of days ahead so I'll be certain to be here and say what day you're coming and I'll meet you at Tours station. This place is ten kilometers out in the country. You can get back to Paris comfortably by the next evening if you're in a hurry and still have a night and morning here. I warn you I've nothing much to offer in the way of news since I don't want to declare myself much in advance as to the nature of the work I'm now doing. [It was *Mourning Becomes Electra*.] I'm certain you'll like it here. I can promise you a grand lungful of Touraine country air and a spell of peaceful repose—and you can give me the New York news!

All kind regards,
Eugene O'Neill

Eugene O'Neill was then forty-one. "That evening, at Château Plessis, we sat before an open fire in the large, high-ceilinged living room," my father wrote. "Eugene O'Neill talked freely until well past midnight of himself and his writings. His speech was always thorough; it was never hurried."

"If I had any idea," he (O'Neill) said, "that I'd have to repeat myself, that I had to stand still, I'd quit writing plays. I'd call it a day. I write primarily for myself, because it is a pleasure, and it would cease to be that if I started repeating. I could have gone on forever with plays like Anna Christie, or with the expressionism of *The Hairy Ape*, but I'm interested in trying to do better things.

"Now, this new play of mine is the hardest thing I've ever tried. God knows, it's the most ambitious. I've done the first draft. I'll do a second, then lay that aside and start on something else. Later I'll come back to it, and perhaps I may have something. I don't want to talk of its content. That hurt me with Dynamo. I just want to finish it, call a stenographer from Paris, and then mail it to the Guild. I've been at work on it for a year. Carlotta seems to think it's all right." ("Wonderful," was the word Mrs. O'Neill used to me.)

The dramatist-son of a grand old actor sipped his Coca-Cola and sat gazing the burning wood chunks.

"I've been remarkably lucky, I think, in the matter of actors.

My mother, whose stage name was Joan Marlowe, and married name is Joan Marlowe Rahe, was in the play "Mr. and Mrs. North" at the Belasco Theatre just east of the Hudson in the early 1940's. The play was later turned into an early TV series centered around a glamorous husband-and-wife crime solving team. My mother went on to co-found the Theatre Information Bulletin in 1944 which she ran with the late Betty Blake for close to a half century.

Certainly the performance of Walter Huston in *Desire Under the Elms* was tremendous. Exactly what I had in mind. And there were splendid performances by Paul Robeson in The Emperor Jones and by Lynn Fontanne in *Strange Interlude.*"

We rode the next day in his Bugatti racer and got it up to 106 kilometers an hour. We swam in his concrete pool and wandered over his forty acres, with his Gordon setter and Dalmatians coming along. Never one for chatter, Eugene O'Neill, but on this beautiful morning in the Touraine he talked rather constantly.

"I love it here," he said simply. "But I've never had any idea of living here permanently. No nonsense about renouncing America. There's such a thing as being sensibly patriotic."

Despite O'Neill's gloomy assessment of the world, sixteen years later the Broadway theater bounced back from its pre-World War II doldrums. His own professional triumph had contributed to the artistic growth of the post-war years.

Joan Marlowe and the late Betty Blake, who were co-publishers and co-editors of the *Theater Information Bulletin* for nearly 50 years, talked of the health and vitality of the theater in their 1954 publication, *Broadway—Inside the Last Decade*. Here are some of their findings and I quote them verbatim:

Cary Grant co-starred in Frank Capra's film version of the Hudson's hit play "Arsenic and Old Lace," which orginally opened in 1941. In the movie, Raymond Massey replaced Boris Karloff who played the sinister nephew on stage.

"Since April of 1944, when the theater in New York was enjoying boom times as a result of the World War II influx, through this last season, we have listed over 2,500 plays which have been optioned for Broadway (the name allocated to that expendable mid-town section where professional theater activity centers). Of these, 770 opened.

This figure of 770 opening nights includes all regular Broadway shows plus New York City Center and American National Theatre and Academy productions but omits 22 foreign language plays brought to this country from abroad, and Off-Broadway fare unless transferred to Broadway houses. Of this number, 60 ran more than a year, 65 closed after 5 performances or less and 4 compliant managements opened and closed the same night.

121 closed after out-of-town tryouts had convinced the powers-that-be of the necessity for further revisions, cast replacements or both. (Only 14 ever re-opened.)

THE BEST AND THE WORST

Comparatively few plays that managed to reach a first night audience were greeted with unanimous acclaim by the critics. Perhaps Arthur Miller's *Death of a Salesman* in 1949 drew the most exciting headlines with one reviewer announcing, "A Great Play Is Born"; another, "Audience Spellbound by Prize Play of 1949"; and others describing it as "Triumphant," "Emotional Dynamite,"

"Powerful," and "A Fine Play, Beautifully Produced and Acted." Among others to inspire critical eloquence were Tennessee Williams's *The Glass Menagerie*, the glorious *South Pacific*, and the current Pulitzer Prize winner, *The Teahouse of the August Moon*. Amazing to note that many recognized smash-hits were not accorded uniformly pro-reviews. But who remembered, after 1,775 performances, that Mary Chase's *Harvey* was dismissed by one critic with something more antagonistic than a mere shrug?

There can be little question in theatrical chronicles, however, that a comedy called *Grandma's Diary* in 1948 received the worst panning of the period. "Ouch!" topped one review; "The Worst Ever," and "She Never Should've Put It in Writing," "The Most Dismal Event of the Sad New Season," "Opened by Mistake," and one critic even left out the actors' names "as decent newspapers omit names of juvenile delinquents."

TWO RAN 10 YEARS

Of the plays on Broadway in 1944, two have been on the boards somewhere ever since; one, the revolutionary *Oklahoma!* and the other, *Good Night,Ladies*, both of which closed for a summer recess after extensive touring. The latter might very well be labeled the most successful flop of the decade, having been soundly trounced by the New York critics, those in the hinterlands and everybody else except the box office queues from coast to coast.

With all its history, with all its great theatrical triumphs, with all its architectural grandeur, one might think a theater like the Hudson would disdain anyone trodding its boards other than the great thespians of the day. But the Hudson, as it showed by welcoming radio to its stage, has always had a bit of a wild streak, a tendency to flirt with newfangled things. When it came to the new medium of television, the theatrics got pretty wild indeed. Just ask Jack Paar and Steve Allen.

11

Live TV, Kate Smith, *Steve Allen's Tonight Show* and Elvis

Ironically, Irving Berlin, who lived in a townhouse on West 46th Street in the 1920's and purchased the Music Box Theatre on 45th Street with just some of his earnings, had the widest exposure for his talent at the Hudson, thanks to Kate Smith.

"I was an entertainer for about a year and then I went uptown and, before long, I was writing songs with a drawing account of $25 a week," Berlin told my father in an interview once. "I'd really had an easy time as a kid, honest. My struggles didn't actually begin until after I'd written *Alexander's Ragtime Band*. It's been a struggle ever since to keep success going. The toughest thing about success is that you've got to keep on being a success. Some day I will reach for it and it won't be there. ..."

God Bless America along with *White Christmas* are among Irving Berlin's most popular tunes' and no one gave *God Bless America* more exposure than Kate Smith. Her famous rendition of Berlin's *God Bless America* made her synonymous with patriotism and American family values. Steve Allen and Jack Paar may have put the Hudson Theatre in the national television audience's way, but Kate Smith was first to cultivate this audience with her show at the Hudson. She hosted a variety show called *The Kate Smith Hour* at the Hudson Theatre from 1950 to 1954. It was an afternoon variety show and was so popular that NBC moved her to prime-time on Wednesday evenings for the

Kate Smith Evening Hour. But the former Broadway musical comedy actress, who was featured in *Hit the Deck* and *Flying High*, achieved her most lasting success when she sang *God Bless America* in 1938 and then over and over again until she died. She got to sing it for millions in the Irving Berlin patriotic movie *This Is the Army*. She sang it last at a bicentennial special on July 4, 1976; ten years later she died in Raleigh, North Carolina. Even the Philadelphia Flyers of the National Hockey League, for a season in the late 1970's, came to depend on Kate and her always-moving rendition of that song to keep their hot streak alive by coming out on the ice before games to belt one out.

Singer Karen Ciacia, who is married to John "Cha Cha" Ciacia (an actor, restaurateur, former fight promoter for Tony Danza, and affectionately known as the "Unofficial Mayor of Little Italy), will be starring in an Off-Broadway bound musical about Kate Smith. "Kate Smith was a pioneer, a woman pioneer for radio and television. She really came out in 1948 and started her show in 1950. It was a big show for four years," Ms. Ciacia told me in an interview.

"She beat out Amos 'n Andy. ... Her manager, Ted Collins, told her if you're going to go up against anyone, go up against the best—and she went past them," Ms. Ciacia continued. "Long before this she was on Broadway for four years, when she was in her 20's. In 1931 she met Ted Collins, the man who would become her manager. The musical she was in that year was *Flying High* and it was the number one musical of that year. When she met Ted Collins, he said, 'Radio is where you belong,' and he was a vice-president of the Columbia Broadcasting System, and he got her a fifteen-minute spot, and she was a phenomenon!"

The *Tonight Show with Steve Allen* ran Mondays to Fridays on NBC, but after Friday, June 15, 1956, Allen stopped hosting the Monday and Tuesday shows to spend more time on his new *The Steve Allen Show* which aired on Sunday nights from 8 to 9 p.m. opposite *The Ed Sullivan Show* on CBS.

"Steve Allen was the quintessential child of vaudeville and, true to the cliché, sometimes slept in a steamer trunk," Robert Metz wrote in his book *The Tonight Show*. "On stage his mother and father, billed as Montrose and Allen, did their comedy act. Deprived of the kind of

Elvis hated when Steve Allen asked him to sing "You Ain't Nothing But a Hound Dog" to an actual hound dog on stage at the Hudson Theatre but the stunt helped gained him national exposure. AP/WIDE WORLD PHOTOS

home life most children take for granted, Steve craved attention to an unusual degree."

Allen's success as host of *Tonight* after his apprenticeship on radio and TV game shows changed him dramatically. Metz says when he started on the show he was "a shy and self-effacing young man." But the author quotes Skitch Henderson as saying Allen "took on the aura of a star within a few months," and the more popular *Tonight* became, the more difficult Allen was said to become. He jumped ship to compete with the king of all variety shows, *The Ed Sullivan Show*, ushering the way for what some call the greatest talk show host in the history of TV talk shows—Johnny Carson notwithstanding—Jack Paar.

"As a 'booker of Talent' I, Andy McKay, was with show from Oct. 1955 to January 1957," Mr. McKay said in a "scrapbook" of the *Tonight Show* which was made available for this book. "Steve Allen was the Host, Mondays to Fridays, until Friday, June 15, 1956. Thereafter, he dropped his appearances on Mondays & Tuesdays so that he could concentrate on his new THE STEVE ALLEN SHOW on Sunday nights from 8 to 9 PM opposite the Ed Sullivan show on CBS. Substitute Hosts were used on Mondays & Tuesdays starting on June 18 and 19, 1956. The TONIGHT show with Steve Allen, etc., ended on Friday, Jan. 25, 1957. A new format called TONIGHT: AMERICA AFTER DARK followed on Monday, January 28, 1957."

Ed McMahon, the late Johnny Carson's long-time sidekick, told *Newsweek* that Allen's show was "loose, it wasn't structured. He could put a camera outside the Hudson Theatre and talk to a mounted policeman for five minutes and get comedy."

One hound dog even upstaged the greatest of rock 'n' roll stars. Elvis, hands folded in front of him, looked down on the brown and white spotted pooch perched on a waist-high platform as if awaiting his cue as Elvis sang *You Ain't Nothing But a Hound Dog*. A book called *Elvis Day by Day* (Ballantine Books) says Elvis was upset by Allen's hound dog stunt and was fearful he would be booed off stage.

Only a few years earlier in 1954, Elvis was told he "can't sing" when he tried out for a group called The Song Fellows. The following month, with the greater aspiration of being an electrician, he was earning a dollar an hour as a short-haul truck driver. But 15 years later he signed a contract with what became the Hilton Hotel in Las Vegas for $1 million to work just eight weeks of that year.

Allen's first show at the Hudson set the stage for the star power of this first *Tonight Show* and its heirs. Sammy Davis, Jr., Kim Novak, Bob Hope, Vincent Price and Wally Cox were the first guests. Some of the personalities who were booked by Andy McKay and appeared on the *Tonight Show with Steve Allen* or guest hosts from Oct. 1955 to Jan. 25,

1957, can be found in Appendix D. However, as they are still fond of doing in the land of television, I will provide you with a quick "sneak preview" of some of the more intriguing highlights here.

Steverino certainly had a weakness for great jazz artists, so it's no surprise he invited Ella Fitzgerald and her Trio on his show, or Dizzie Gillespie and his Band or other top jazz performers of the era. But these great artists had to share the dais with Mr. Allen's other guests, drawn seemingly at random from the very heights of world culture to the very depths. Thus Steve might one minute be interviewing a hyper intellectual like *New Yorker* magazine poet Ogden Nash and, the very next minute, be hamming it up with hypnotist "Polgar." Of course Steve had on other top comics like Louis Nye; he also gave his stage and cameras over to the Basque Dancers (Spanish folk dancers) and Elwood Carson (no relation to Johnny, I believe), a "trick cyclist."

Obviously, the eclectic roots of vaudeville ran deep in Mr. Allen, but one wonders what the American viewing public made of this cultural brew. Allen never stuck around long enough for us to find out, and he was superseded by the ultimately suave Jack Paar who made his own show mostly about sophisticated conversation. The "trick cyclist" strain would reemerge with the next host of *Tonight*, Johnny Carson. He, like Allen, seemed to find all strata of culture fascinating—and entertaining. Of course those listed above weren't even the "off beat" acts like spectacles such as Murray Wiener, a collector of odd fishes and animals, or Skip Reiss, purveyor of futuristic hats for men. Then there was Nancy O'Malley, "Queen of the 1955 National Donut Week," and Chick Oklee, who operated a meat cutting school. What these latter two were doing on the program is a true head scratcher, unless Steve was getting the late-night munchies.

A brief history of the Hudson Theatre, prepared for the Millenium Broadway Hotel, talked about the years leading up to the *Steve Allen Show*:

> Needing more room for television production, NBC at one point in time was considering the idea of leasing the Hudson Theatre or the Center in Radio City. The network was not interested in buying but had in mind leasing the space. The space at the Center would require too much reconstruction to make the space feasible

for television production and thus they settled on buying the Hudson.

Negotiations went on for several weeks with the theater's owners before a price was settled on. NBC wanted to lease the theater, as opposed to buying it. However, the owners wanted to sell it. There was an offer that NBC made to lease the theater for three years which was rejected and also a bid of $450,000 was refused. At one time it looked as if none of the negotiations were going to work out for NBC. Mr. Howard S. Cullman, the show backer and a tobacco dealer, is credited with having saved the day by dealing directly with the television network. The Hudson was sold to NBC in June 1950 by playwrights Howard Lindsay and Russel Crouse.

Howard Lindsay and Russel Crouse were hesitant about selling the theater. However, in a joint interview, they claimed that the management of the theater and the production of plays had interfered with their writing of plays. They wanted to get away from being business men in the theater. NBC purchased the Theatre for $595,000 and converted it into a television studio. They owned and operated the theater from 1950-1962. Popular shows such as the very first "Tonight Show" starring Steve Allen and the "Jack Paar Show" were filmed there.

The first nationwide broadcast of the "Tonight Show" occurred on September 27, 1956, with Steve Allen as the host. The premiere included guest stars such as Sammy Davis, Jr., Kim Novak, Vincent Price, Bob Hope, and Wally Cox. Allen showed off his simple set during the broadcast. Depending on the scene, the stage was covered with either cardboard forests or drawing rooms. In his first broadcast, Allen learned how to juggle his show between the two audiences. The New York audience remained live the entire show, while local stations would break for commercials. Therefore, Allen was left on camera trying to amuse the local viewers (in New York) without getting ahead of the national audience. Every break, Allen was forced to backtrack and explain to the national audience what he had been discussing during their commercial break.

The earlier episodes of the "Tonight Show" were dominated primarily by commercials which Allen enacted himself. In one show alone, Allen did promotions for the Polaroid Land Camera,

Extraordinary pianist and night club singer Kathleen Landis, a fixture at the Cafe Pierre in the Pierre Hotel for two decades, fondly remembers working with Steve Allen when she first came to the Big Apple.

Delmonte pineapple juice, Clear Spar Varnish, the book *You Too Can Make a Speech* and S&H Green Stamps.

Kathleen Landis, the Café Pierre's legendary pianist and songstress for the past eighteen years, had a telling as well as amusing run-in with the former king of late night TV when she was still a bit of a greenhorn herself in Manhattan cabaret society.

"I was performing in the Grille Room at the St. Regis Hotel," Ms. Landis recollects, "when one evening I heard a gentleman complimenting my playing. I looked through the dimly lit, smoky room and saw a man with dark glasses having a drink in the back. He then asked me to play *Body and Soul*, a standard in the jazz repertoire. When I finished the set, he asked me to join him at his table. The year was 1983 and next to the Grille Room (which used to be the room where Mabel Mercer sang with Jimmy Lyons on piano) was the famous 'King Cole Room' that proudly displayed the Maxfield Parrish painting of the 1920's of King Cole and his court characters. The room was famous for the acts it presented in dinner theater format.

"I was vaguely aware that a new act had just come in titled 'Seymour Glick Is Alive But Sick and Living in New York.' The show was starring its creator—Steve Allen—a man my parents watched on television. I knew his name because I had always heard how smart he was from them. Well, as I sat down to join my up-to-now-unrecognized admirer, I gasped, 'My mother would be thrilled!' I'm sure that was a great boost to his ego. So we talked for a few minutes about his show coming in, which of course was a farce on 'Jacques Brel Is Alive and Well,' but soon the topic of songwriters and lyrics became the focus. He was interested in how someone as young as myself had discovered Alec Wilder. I explained that Jimmy Lyons who was my New York mentor had played Wilder's music for Mabel Mercer and he was still playing at night at the Waldorf. At that time I only knew a few, but they were ones that Allen particularly liked—*Blackberry Winter* was his favorite.

"He came back regularly after or in between his shows and just sat quietly and listened while sipping a wine. He asked me if I would like to play some of his original material and I was enthusiastic to try it. The next day at least three volumes of published material arrived by messenger. Wanting to impress him positively, I got to work right away and the next time he came in I played five or so songs, including *This Could Be the Start of Something Big*, his most played song, and *Mainly a State of Mind*. He was delighted and that evening he asked if I would like to play a warm-up set before the show started— of course of his original songs. It was a challenge because I had to learn them so fast and find tempo changes and segues for them. I think I eventually had around thirty of his in the medley. He asked me what I would charge and I gave him a ridiculously low price of $25 per pre-show.

"I played every night throughout the show's stay and he paid me when he came in. The last night of the show he didn't come in and didn't say goodbye. He also didn't pay me the last $25—I was a little disappointed in him because of that until that Christmas and many following when he would send me a card with his picture and Jane Meadow's. That made up for the missing payment and then some. I sent that first card on to my mother who prized it among her valuables. I still have all his music and now and then include some numbers in my performances at the Café Pierre. I stop and think about how multi-talented he was and what a lovely opportunity he offered me as a new performer in the big city."

NBC's extraordinarily popular daytime game show *The Price Is Right*, hosted by Bill Cullen, premiered at the Hudson on November 26, 1956. One of the most popular shows on TV, it offered unusual prizes to contestants who could most accurately guess how much something cost. The winning bidder on a grand piano, a Texas farmer, won a baby elephant as a bonus. Spurning the pachyderm's $4,000 "equivalent value," he forced the show to fly in an elephant from Kenya. Other outlandish prizes included 100 pounds of Swiss cheese and a 1928 chauffeur-driven Rolls Royce.

William Laurence Cullen, who died in 1990, was born in Pittsburgh and got his start in broadcasting as an unpaid announcer for WWSU in that U.S. steel capital. "I'm happy if the contestants win and I'm upset if they lose," he once told an interviewer. "I am the timing. I am the pace. I speed it up. I play it down. I make it flow. It's a challenge. ... It's great to be witty and funny, but a host should never distract a contestant from winning money."

Rod Roddy was one of his announcers. On a personal note, Joey Reynolds, a close friend of Roddy's and talk show host of late-night radio's *Joey Reynolds Show*, gave me a literal car trunk load of clothes Roddy had once worn. When I lost weight I had to give them to someone else. But they were as fine as some of the gifts on *The Price Is Right*, luxurious and expensively-tailored.

When Steve Allen was tapped to host NBC-TV's Sunday night *The Steve Allen Show*, to try to compete with *The Ed Sullivan Show* on CBS at the same time slot, the network had a problem filling Allen's shoes as he stopped hosting the Monday and Tuesday *Tonight* shows. If anyone could fill all slots it was Allen who was and still is known after his death as "the man who can do it all." He was a songwriter, actor, TV host, pianist extraordinaire, you name it.

For the first Monday and Tuesday without Allen, June 18th and 19th, NBC got General DeWitt to host *Tonight*. For the 25th and 26th, Al Capp, the cartoonist, and Gene Rayburn, who would go on to become one of TV's all-time great game show hosts, co-hosted. But for the Fourth of July they got a relatively unknown radio host and actor named Jack Paar to host, and Paar was asked to sub again on September 3rd and 4th.

Tony Randall, who had made a name for himself in movies, was a much more frequent host. But Paar ended up being, by at least some industry estimates, the all-time king of late-night talk, Johnny Carson included.

"The positioning of Steve Allen against CBS on Sunday by NBC is ironical," *Billboard* wrote (April 21, 1956) "because the performer was originally brought East from Hollywood by CBS. After giving him a few chances on shows, CBS gave up on him, and NBC then signed him to a contract. And it has been at NBC where he has made his mark as a performer." *Billboard* added that "Allen's stock has risen greatly in the trade this year what with his other activities in motion pictures, records and writing. His latest stint is as a columnist for *Cosmopolitan*."

One of Steve Allen's biggest coups was getting Elvis Presley on his show on Sunday, July 1, 1956, just as Elvis' career began to skyrocket. Elvis was in Savannah, Georgia, on Monday, June 25th; and the next day at the Coliseum in Charlotte, North Carolina, he talked openly and honestly to a local reporter about where his kind of music came from.

"The colored folks' been singing it and playing it just like I'm doin' now, man, for more years than I know. They played it like that in the shanties and in their juke joints, and nobody paid it no mind 'til I goosed it up. I got it from them. Down in Tupelo, Mississippi, I used to hear old Arthur Crudup bang his box the way I do now, and I said if I ever got to the place where I could feel all old Arthur felt, I'd be a music man like nobody ever saw." Two days later there are headlines in newspapers across the country that say Elvis "Bites Hand of Girl Reporter." Actually, he gently and jokingly nibbled her fingers during an interview. On Friday, June 29th, Elvis did a rehearsal for his upcoming Sunday appearance on *The Steve Allen Show*. He did a gig in Richmond, Virginia, the night before, climbing aboard a train back to New York after the Richmond show. On stage at the Hudson, Elvis began with *I Want You, I Need You, I Love You*. He then sang *Hound Dog*, which he didn't record until the next day at the nearby RCA Studio, singing to that basset hound. The same night Elvis appeared on *Gardner Calling!*, a popular late-night live interview show, a precursor of *The Jack Paar Show*. Gardner tried to put him on the spot by asking him if he'd learned anything from those who'd criticized his music for being too wild or unsavory. "No, I haven't," he told Gardner. "I don't feel like I'm doing anything wrong." Discussing his effect on teenagers, Elvis reiterated what he'd been saying all along: "I don't see how any type of music would have any bad influence on people when it's only music. ... I mean, how would rock 'n' roll music make anyone rebel against their parents?" It is his sleepy-eyed, almost doped-up appearance, though, almost certainly a conscious evocation of James Dean, that leaves the most lasting impression.

Jack Paar substituted as a host on the *Tonight Show* sporadically as did Tony Randall. But as ratings plummeted, affected by the advent of quality prime-time popular series, NBC executives hit on another scheme which turned out to be one of the most hair-brained in the history of live TV. Moving weeknight operation of *Tonight* from the Hudson Theatre to the RCA Exhibition Hall in New York City, NBC hired six of the nation's leading columnists, including New York gossip columnist Earl Wilson (of the *New York Post*), "to capture the tempo and pacing of nightlife throughout the country," Norman Frank, who produced the new *Tonight* show, said in a statement at the time. "Since entertainment is so much a part of life in *America After Dark*, [the name of the new show], highlights of the entertainment world will be a regular feature. The format will remain flexible enough to allow NBC television cameras to go anywhere for *Tonight* live coverage of newsworthy events and specialties dealing with 'Nighttime, USA.'"

"The new *Tonight* format will have us making backstage visits to theaters and nightclubs to talk with top personalities. We'll showcase new talent, attend parties and venture into any phase of nighttime activity that is technically feasible," Frank said. Legendary columnist Bob Considine, who was with the International News Service at the time, and Vernon Scott, the Hollywood reporter for United Press, later United Press International, did some of the new duties.

Not long after, NBC was very fortunate indeed to be rescued from these well-intentioned but floundering late night efforts by that most superlative of on-air conversationalists, Mr. Jack Paar. The whole difference between radio and TV was supposed to be the images. Why would anyone *watch* someone *talk* on television? Paar, working out of the Hudson Theatre, would show them all.

12

Jack Paar

On July 29, 1957, television history was made once again at the Hudson Theatre. Jack Parr's *Tonight Show* aired on NBC. Audiences tuned in to see what Paar, emotional and sometimes testy, would do next as much as for his occasional celebrity guests.

The first two years of the *Tonight Show* under Paar's reign were at the Hudson after which the show moved to NBC's Rockefeller Center Studios.

Paar was blunt about what he thought about the physical condition of the Hudson Theatre. Aside from badly needing renovation, it was, he said, "much too large for an intimate, conversational program." Yet the program worked—and how. Paar had one particularly strong run-in with one of the NBC exec's on the show. The executive was removed and at Paar's urging the two heads of NBC, Bob Sarnoff and Bob Unter, said, Paar relates in his autobiography, "They would withdraw network people from the show and ... I should form my own staff and produce *Tonight*."

Sarnoff actually grew to be so happy with the *Tonight Show* that in its second year with Paar, he had its name changed to *The Jack Paar Show*. As *The Jack Parr Show* became increasingly successful, Paar had to be more particular about whom he booked. When a Broadway press agent tried to book an unknown English actor in a modestly well-reviewed play, Paar remembered asking, "What would he talk about?" The actor was Peter Ustinov who went on to become internationally famous and a friend of Paar's for twenty-five years.

Jack Paar's hosting of the *Tonight Show* at the Hudson seemed pro-

Jack Parr, who some believe was the greatest TV talk show host in history, entertained the troops during the Second World War and did a lot of radio prior to NBC hiring him to replace Steve Allen. Here he enjoys a laugh with Richard Nixon on the set of his TV show at the Hudson. PHOTO BY CORBIS

grammed to fail from the start. The man who was to become thought of as the world's greatest conversationalist almost wasn't. He had been called in to fix the impossible after taking over *The Morning Show* on CBS from Walter Cronkite. (Paar's own brother had written a letter to CBS stating that, "We enjoyed Walter Cronkite so much and hated to see him leave.")

Paar himself is fairly amusing about the uneven beginning of the show. "There were many problems before the program went on the air," Paar writes in his book *P.S., Jack Paar*, "and the first was the director who was assigned to me. He came from *The Ernie Kovacs Show* but, although he was talented technically, he did not understand what I had in mind.

"I overheard him one day say that he would 'book the show,' and I would just come in and do it. The first thing he did was to suggest to the staff a guest who had the longest toenail in the world. The man had to walk around with a box over his foot to protect his fame. Of course, he was cancelled by me immediately."

Paar continues about the Hudson specifically, and not especially flatteringly:

> "The program was broadcast live each night for one hour and forty-five minutes, Monday through Friday, from the Hudson Theatre on West Forty-fourth Street. The Hudson was a broken down, depressing place, much too large for an intimate, conversational program.
>
> "The small staff I brought with me to the program were old friends and very loyal ones. There were about five of us who had to combat the lower echelon of NBC minor executives. One serious problem with the NBC people was that they simply didn't understand that people talking could be interesting and entertaining. They wanted movement, dancing, and burlesque bits. On [our] budget we could hardly afford half of the Smothers Brothers.
>
> "The main problem was with an executive who had previously 'created' *America After Dark* and wanted to 'create' something again. He was not well and would frequently go into what would be termed medically as epileptic seizures. This would usually happen in private. We kept it from the staff and NBC until it became so serious I never knew when an attack would be brought on by stress or by his drinking, which he was not supposed to do. How in the hell can you run a program of one hour and forty-five minutes of live television every night and not have stress?
>
> "For the first two years, when the program came from the Hudson Theatre on West Forty-fourth Street, I had a private office down the block at the famous Algonquin Hotel. The Algonquin was, and still is, the gathering place of the theatrical and literary life of Manhattan. It is in this hotel's dining room that Alexander Woollcott, Robert Benchley, Dorothy Parker, George S. Kaufman, Marc Connelly, Tallulah Bankhead and Oscar Levant would meet for lunch and formed the famous Round Table. All those of the above who were still living in the Sixties later appeared on the program."

While Paar credited Johnny Carson for taking the *Tonight Show* to "historic heights," his own two years at the Hudson may have set the standard for live talk TV. He continues in his book:

"I usually had dinner there before the show, and one night dining with a few friends I found myself in an eyelock with Noël Coward. I felt awkward because I could see that he recognized me from television and was getting up to come to our table. I thought, "Dear God, I hope I am wrong." I had nothing to say at all to Noël Coward, so I looked down at the dinner plate only to find the brass buttons on his blazer cuff at the level of my coffee. Looking up I was embarrassed, flattered, and tried to stand, but he said, "Please don't let me interrupt your dinner. I just want to say that I am amazed how you do that program every night and I am addicted to it. We have nothing like it in England. I have become a fan of yours." He later came on the program and we became friends until he died.

Paar made his talk show look easy. It was anything but. The program, he said, was "described then as an hour and forty-five minutes of people sitting around and trying to change the subject." "I called it a night light to the bathroom," he said. ... "In the first two years of live broadcasts from the Hudson Theatre, our show presented for the first time to a national audience the following: Carol Burnett, the Smothers Brothers, Mike Nichols and Elaine May, Bob Newhart, Alex King, Shelley Berman, Phyllis Diller, Peggy Cass, Charlie Weaver, Don Rickles, Louis Nye and many others."

Paar was the first to introduce television audiences to Nipsey Russell, Godfrey Cambridge, Bill Cosby and Dick Gregory—"all of whom could and did out-talk me," he once said, "the king of white talkers!"

"I have a confession to make," Paar continued in his book. "Hundreds of young performers wanted to sing on the show or dance or do their comedy routines, but the big-status thing became sitting and talking with me. Many felt badly if they did their acts and left to great applause but were not asked over to the davenport."

For his part, Paar endeared himself to some hard-boiled NBC executives with his unusually self-effacing style. It may have masked a

Legendary TV talk show host Joe Franklin (r) joins Laura Belle Bundy, the star of "Legally Blond: the Musical," and Joel Vig, Ms. Bundy's co-star in the musical "Hairspray" at a book party for "Broadway After Dark," by the author of this book and his late father, Ward Morehouse. Franklin says part of Jack Paar's appeal was his personal unpredictability on screen. "Everyone was waiting for what Jack Paar was going to do next," he says. PHOTO BY ROSE BILLINGS

huge ego but it also had great audience appeal. He even had one guest, a John Reddy, Jr., read a critique on the air.

Talk show host Joe Franklin, the undisputed "King of Nostalgia," remembered that the Hudson and Paar were cut from the same "gentile" cloth. "The Hudson was a gentile theater and in his own mind Jack Paar was a gentile guy," Franklin told me. "My dream was to get him on the TV panel with Jack Benny. I had Jack Benny on several times. I had Jack Paar on several times. I wanted to have them on together. He was proud of the fact that when he was Jack Benny's summer replacement around 1940 he got almost as high a rating as Jack Benny. And Jack Benny was the king of all. And he used to brag that when he took over the variety show from Steve Allen in 1957, *The Tonight Show* was carried on some 40 stations and he used to brag about the fact he took it to over 170 stations."

"The big phrase all over the world was, 'what is Jack Paar really like?' He was electric," Franklin continued. "He was very edgy. He was boastful—and that boasting was justified. And you know what his famous phrase was? 'I kid you not.' The whole world would say, 'I kid you not.' The whole world would watch Jack Paar and the next morn-

Martin Riskin, who has been a top executive with The Waldorf-Astoria, The Plaza Hotel and the Pierre Hotel, is seen here at a hotel gala with Marc Chagall. Riskin said the Broadway Millennium has the great advantage of having a Broadway theater for shows and major special events, including gala's like those held there by the Theatre Museum and the American Place Theatre.

ing the conversation was, 'who was on with Jack Paar last night?' ... "On *The Jack Paar Show* the guests were secondary. He was the guy. ... He used to say about living in America that 'in America you don't have to be a star if you don't want to.' That was his famous line. He was on with me many times after he retired."

Warren Wexler, former press representative for the New York Real Estate Board, notes about Paar, whom he was a great fan of, "I think one of the qualities that drew people to him was his unpredictability. ... someone who didn't have a tight reign on his emotions and you never knew when something would set him off. I knew the NBC censor criticized him for using the word 'water closet' on the air and he walked off. A lot of the people he had on didn't have much of a reputation in show business but they were appealing talkers.

"Another interesting thing is how those early talk shows overcame the movies. People stopped watching the movies on TV and started watching them—people conversing with each other—which seemed less inherently dramatic."

Joe Franklin told me about one close friend of his who recalled, "I talked to Jack Paar long after Paar's show was over. They were talking about love affairs and those whom one would have liked to be the love of one's life.

"I said 'Tell me, Jack,' and I smiled because I knew he had a sense of humor. 'Who would you say would be the love of your life?' So he thought for a minute and then he said, 'Judy Holliday.' Now to the average person who would hear that, they would say, 'what an odd combination—the intellectual Jack Paar and the ditzy blond Judy was known to play. He said in life Judy was a very intellectual lady."

"Jack Paar was a broadcaster—everyone was 'broad' in those days," Joey Reynolds, host of the long-running (10 years and counting) *The Joey Reynolds Show,* the highly rated, nationally syndicated late-night radio show broadcasting from WOR Studios in New York, told me. "Now, it's narrow. The question you're asking me is whether he will be remembered? I have to answer you in what demographic? Because that's what we've done—we've segmented everybody. ... We've separated people so definitely that we've kept out anyone who doesn't have an interest. The disadvantage of blogging and internet-scaping is that we don't know where to go. All special interests. It's like you need a lobbyist or guide. And in those days, that's what Jack Paar was. He was a guide. That's what he did. You would rely on him for all of these things that you are now experiencing on your own. ..."

"Steve Allen, Jack Paar and Johnny Carson all come from radio," Joey Reynolds continued, "which is an interactive medium before the internet. Those days are gone. The new generation of talk show hosts come from 'stand-up'—and they are used to doing it 'one-way.' Conan O'Brien is a stand-up comic. He's very good at writing and he's good at jokes ... the same with Letterman. It doesn't make them bad—it is only a style. They don't come from interactive ... it's a skill to listen. But you don't get that off stand-up comedy. Jack Paar was not a stand-up comic, he was a monologist. That means he would hear something and report his version of it to you while at the same time listen to others talk and let them speak. That style doesn't exist now. I'm doing it—I stole it."

Mr. Reynolds also has fond memories of Jack Paar's predecessor, Steve Allen: "There's a story that tells it like it is with Steve Allen. You know he lived in Beverly Hills and had a Japanese gardener. So Steve's a workaholic. He's got files under his arm, he's carrying some music and he's probably juggling with his foot—and he's got the car key case in his mouth, and he's walking out to get into his car and the gardener says, 'hello' and Steve says 'ulow' with the keys in his mouth. That's Steve!"

Dody Goodman was the closest thing Paar ever had to a co-host. I went up to see the now-elderly Goodman, who was in good spirits and without any seemingly great loss of memory, in her Upper West Side apartment.

"That's where Jack Paar started, at the Hudson Theatre," Goodman recalled. "That's where we all started. It was an old theater that was not being used. ... I did a play there. ... How could I not love him. He gave me the best job I'd ever had. And I knew he did not love me. ... I thought he did many things against me."

Goodman told me that Paar rightly or wrongly believed she was becoming a co-host, and he didn't want that so he eventually let her go even though she continued to get paid according to her contract. "He was a very complicated person. I think he liked what I did."

When Jack Paar was first interviewing Dody Goodman for his show, Robet Metz writes in *The Tonight Show*, she rambled on and on. Paar, as amused as he was mildly exasperated, finally asked her, Metz says, "Are you for real? Or are you putting me on?" Metz continues to quote Paar as saying, "She twisted her mouth, patted the top of her pink hair, widened her eyes and said, 'A little!'" Ironically, Dody was in a revival of *Born Yesterday* which originally starred Judy Holliday.

Paar walked off the show in 1960 after learning the NBC censors had bleeped the word "water closet" from his telecast. He told viewers, "I am leaving *The Tonight Show*. There must be a better way of making a living than this." He quit the show permanently in 1962 then during the next three years hosted a weekly prime-time variety show. The broadcast show that aired on February 28, 1964, was a sort of reprise of his nightly TV show with some of the old regulars including Dody Goodman. That night Paar began the show with a one-liner after the applause died down. "Thank you very much," he said "All that for little me. Mr. Show Business."

Paar introduced Goodman as an "old, old friend." "She came on the second night of '*The Tonight Show*' ... She's stage struck; she comes to New York to audition and forgets for what." Goodman talked about the first time she was on his show and of some of the disastrous blind dates she had. One of them was so tall he could barely reach down to kiss her good night. She told of having a date with a guy who was very rich. "We used to have candlelight dinners, caviar, champagne, the whole bit. He had just celebrated his 93rd birthday." She also admitted that she always kissed her dates goodnight as it "kept them from feeling rejected."

Comedian Godfrey Cambridge was a guest that same night. One of his favorite topics was rising to the middle class. As a boy he lived in a tenement that was in deplorable condition. "You know, the ceiling falls and hits you in the head and you say, 'put on your helmet, here it comes!'" he said.

Superstar singer-actress Diahann Carroll was one of Paar's many guests who gives Paar credit for boosting her career tremendously, she told audiences at her 2007 show at Feinstein's, New York's premier nightclub at the Regency Hotel named after singer-pianst Michael Feinstein.

Julie Wilson certainly had a memorable night appearing on Paar's show—albeit without Jack Paar. As she recollects: "The night I went on *The Jack Paar Show* he went to London and the wonderful woman from *What's My Line?*, Arlene Francis, was the emcee. I think I had been touring in a show with a dear friend of hers, and she told Arlene I did my yoga exercises everyday, which I did. So when I got to the show Arlene said when the commercial goes out, 'come over to my chair, in front of my desk and do a head stand.' I said, 'I don't have a leotard on and I don't know if it'll be proper.' She said, 'Well, don't say anything—just get up and do it.' So I did it, putting my dress (the bottom of it) between my ankles to hold it and then the band started up and I started to move a little too much and my dress dropped and there I was in my pantyhose and my expensive dress was over my head ... and the camera swerved away and that was one of those funny bloopers!"

Jack Paar may not have been a big supporter of Dody Goodman or of the Hudson but, while Ms. Goodman may have needed him, the Hudson did not. The theater would find other suitors in the years to come—when Broadway itself was reeling financially from the effects of that little, glowing tube now in everyone's home—that little, glowing tube that Paar had learned to master like no one before him.

13

Strange Interlude: Broadway Returns to the Hudson

Because of new changes in ownership of the theater, the 1960's once again brought great theatrical acclaim to the Hudson starting with the production of *Toys in the Attic* starring Maureen Stapleton, Irene Worth and Jason Robards, which opened on February 25, 1960, and ran 464 performances.

"Lillian Hellman's new drama, which opened last night at the Hudson Theatre, is a case of Southern decadence that makes Tennessee Williams's famous probings into the subject seem almost gently whimsical," wrote Richard Watts, Jr. in the *New York Post*. Jason Robards, Jr., as a pathetic, foolish, tempestuous brother who returns home with his pockets stuffed with cash, headed a stellar cast that included Maureen Stapleton, Ann Revere and Irene Worth. "There isn't a performance that seems short of perfection," noted Watts.

A revival of Eugene O'Neill's *Strange Interlude*, with Geraldine Page and Jane Fonda, opened at the Hudson three years later on March 11, 1963, and ran 104 performances. It can be truly said that with that production, the Actors Studio outdid itself. It was, after all, the studio's first production by its Actors Studio Theatre. The play, said *New York Times* critic Howard Taubman, "abounds in dramatic moments that make the stage a place of magic." Director José Quintero didn't employ the play's original device of having the characters voice their secret thoughts as asides. He instead incorporated these thoughts into the dialogue.

Famed TV actor Richard Thomas as a child played the part of Gordon Evans. One-time movie idol Franchot Tone, Ben Gazzara and Geraldine Page were also featured. "Ben Gazzara, always a dynamic actor, is brilliant," Richard Watts, Jr. said in the *Post*. The first act alone of the production ran for four-plus hours, and the audience was given time for a snack or even dinner; it was the first of several productions to open on Broadway in subsequent years that ran marathon lengths. Jane Fonda, who played the role of Madeline Arnold, was singled out by several critics for her excellent performance.

Renowned acting teacher Terry Schreiber remembers seeing Eugene O'Neill's *Strange Interlude* at the Hudson. I present his recollections as he gave them to me:

> I remember with great anticipation getting tickets for *Strange Interlude*. In college O'Neill had been my God. I even hitchhiked from St. Paul, Minnesota, in the summer of 1957 mainly to see *Long Day's Journey into Night* on Broadway and the revival of *The Iceman Cometh* down at the old 'Circle in the Square' on Bleecker Street.
>
> A buddy of mine hitchhiked with me and in two nights we saw ten hours of O'Neill. Standing on a street corner in the Village after *Iceman*, I turned to my friend and said, How about a drink? He looked at me in awe, replying, After ten hours of boozed up men and women, you want a drink? You've got to be crazy! I don't care if I never have another drink in my life! I would still go to an O'Neill play with the same eager enthusiasm as when I went to the above two classics. When the Actors' Studio production of the nine-hour *Strange Interlude* was announced, I was one of the first in line. I had gotten an A+ on a paper I had written on the play for an English assignment in college. The role of Nina, O'Neill's classic 'wife, mistress, mother, whore,' fascinated me. The ideal casting for me would have been Kim Stanley but she was busy doing Masha in the Actor's Studio production of *Three Sisters*. However, I gladly accepted Geraldine Page in the role. I have vivid memories

of Ben Gazzara, Pat Hingle, William Prince and Franchot Tone and Jane Fonda in small cameo roles.

If memory serves, the evening began promptly at 5:00 p.m. I think there was a dinner break from 6:30 to 7:30. I believe the curtain came down around 11:30. I remember particularly that before the dinner break Ben Gazzara seemed to be walking through the role of Edmund Darrel but, after the dinner break, whether it was food or a good shot of scotch, he really caught on fire. It was a memorable evening for me at the Hudson, a very special evening of a rarely produced O'Neill classic. Far better than the stiff and tedious British production that followed a few years later.

Since my arrival in New York in 1960 I spent many other evenings enjoying plays in a grand old theater—the Hudson. My memory of the Hudson is of a smaller house than a lot of the "new Broadway Barns" when drama, and a smaller cast, could still produce an intimate production in a seemingly intimate environment.

The drama on stage was equaled or surpassed by the drama swirling around the Hudson off stage. Seymour Durst sold the Hudson and adjacent properties to the United States Steel and Carnegie Pension Fund and then leased it back, hoping to develop it. Faced with a downturn in the real estate market the pension fund eventually hired William Dwyer to manage the Hudson. After a court battle, Dwyer succeeded in ousting the pornography operator and the Hudson started showing mainstream films. The curtain rises on this entire topsy-turvy and, at times, unsavory period in the next chapter.

14

"*Titanic* II" Avoided: Hudson Saved From Wrecking Ball

During the 1960's, '70's and early '80's, the Hudson seemed perpetually on the verge of meeting its own version of Henry B. Harris's fate aboard the *Titanic*.

In late 1965, Abraham Hirshfeld, a millionaire Manhattan garage owner, bought the theater with the idea of turning it into a garage as had been done with other historic Times Square theaters. But a stream of negative press greeted the announcement of his plans. Actors, producers and the press joined the bandwagon to save the Hudson. My father was among these supporters. He devoted one of his *Broadway After Dark* columns to sing its praises—faced with the "quite unthinkable" possibility it was going to be raised and replaced by a garage:

> Every Broadway theater has its own personality; its associations through the years stay in the memory. The Empire, which has vanished, is linked with the productions of Charles Frohman. The Music Box is Irving Berlin's playhouse and the Shubert is actually the Sam S. Shubert Theatre, named for the young showman from Syracuse who died in a train wreck in Pennsylvania in 1905.
>
> And there's the Hudson, the oldest drama stand in town with the exception of the Lyceum. The report that the Hudson is to be con-

verted into a garage has brought wails of protest from people who care about the state of the theater. There've been tears in the eyes of members of The Lambs who have appeared in Hudson presentations. Located in 44th Street, just across the thoroughfare, they will tell you that the Hudson is a playhouse of honorable antiquity.

It was at the Hudson that Alfred Lunt had a year-long frolic in Booth Tarkington's *Clarence* and there that Ethel Barrymore first spoke these cryptic words, "That's all there is, there isn't any more."

Margaret Anglin had a two-week engagement in *Camille*; Paul Armstrong, writing two and three plays a season during the first decade of the century, supplied *The Heir to the Hoorah* which had a fair engagement, and the Hudson got a fine run with Bernard Shaw's *Man and Superman*.

The Hudson also went in for Clyde Fitch's play, *Her Sister*, and it's not at all surprising to know that the beloved Lucile Watson was in the cast.

The list could go on. All of us are shocked to be told the Hudson may become a garage. It's quite unthinkable.

This was not the first time developers threatened to turn the Hudson into a garage. NBC had sold it in 1961 to Samuel Lehrer, another garage owner, just as a play by Hugh Wheeler, *Look, We've Come Through*, had been scheduled to open there on October 25th of that year.

Robert Whitehead, president of the League of New York Theaters, and Ralph Bellamy, head of Actors' Equity, said NBC had "consigned the Hudson Theatre to the scrap heap." They said the network was "contemptuous of the interest of the theater and the public" and was acting with "irresponsibility." They asked Mayor Robert F. Wagner to intervene.

Whitehead and Bellamy (perhaps best remembered today for being the good-hearted sap in the Cary Grant-Rosalind Russell film *His Gal Friday*) were joined in their protest by producer David J. Cogan who had purchased the Biltmore Theatre from CBS and was restoring it for legitimate play use. Cogan reportedly paid $850,000 for the Biltmore and was spending close to $700,000 on renovations.

"NBC made an energetic effort to find theatrical buyers for the Hudson," a spokesman for the network said at the time, "but none were even remotely competitive in bidding."

Seymour Durst, the developer father of Douglas Durst, briefly owned the Hudson in the late 1960's when "Lillian Valin" bought the historic theater. Sam Zolotow, renowned theater columnist for *The New York Times*, revealed that Lillian Valin was a "dummy corporation" for the elder Durst. Durst had told reporters over these years that the area would only improve after it was developed.

Durst told *The New York Times* that when he owned the Hudson and adjoining properties, including the Lenox Hotel and Blue Ribbon restaurant, rents amounted to $500,000 annually but real estate taxes came to $600,000.

The U.S. Steel and Carnegie Pension Fund bought the theater in 1973, successfully ousting the Avon management which had shown porno films for several years.

Echoing the raid on the Hudson when *The Fight*, which had a scene in a bordello, the New York Supreme Court in December 1972 upheld a 30-day license suspension on the theater. But its manager vowed to keep it operating.

While its darkest days as a porno house (from the late 1960's to early '70's) were over, the theater's owners and management team tried one unsuccessful thing after another to return the theater to a semblance of its heritage.

William T. Dwyer, the rental agents for the Hudson, spent $200,000 renovating the property in 1975 before it reopened in September of that year as a $1 motion picture showplace. It reopened with a double feature of the James Bond movies, *Live and Let Die* and *The Man with the Golden Gun*.

In November 1975 *Variety* announced the Hudson, which had been used as a budget $1 per person second-run movie house for a mere two months, would shift to a first-run house with a film called *The Hiding Place*. But even the attempt to show first-run films was unsuccessful and the Hudson closed on January 15, 1976.

Two years later, it was still dark and *Show Business,* the weekly entertainment newspaper, asked in bold headlines, is it "Unbookable or Jinxed?"

Carol Burnett, seen here with Aldon James (left), president of The National Arts Club, and John James at the National Arts Club, achieved one of her biggest successes in "The Carol Burnett Show" on CBS in the late 1960's and 1970's during some of the darkest days for Times Square and the Hudson Theatre. As Harvey Korman, Vicki Lawrence, Lyle Waggoner and Tim Conway brought laughter into millions of homes Times Square and the Hudson became shadows of their glorious pasts but much brighter days were ahead.
PHOTO BY ROSE BILLINGS

Returning it once again to a legitimate theater seemed one strong possibility. "Assuming that the stage is functional and the dressing rooms useable, it would be fine for a Broadway show," Shubert chairman Gerald Schoenfeld told *Show Business* in February 1978. "The Booth [Theatre] and the Golden [Theatre] have a similar number of seats and they are successfully showing *The Gin Game* and *For Colored Girls*..." Today in 2007 the Shubert Organization owns 17 Broadway playhouses, including half interest with the Irving Berlin estate of the Music Box Theatre. (Three more theaters are in Boston, Philadelphia and Washington D.C.)

The one thing to keep in mind here is that the Hudson was not alone in its struggles. A number of earthshaking events conspired against Broadway during this era. First, as mentioned, television drew away much of Broadway's regular customers. The folks who regularly attended "boulevard comedies" and other middle-brow fare started staying home and watching *Playhouse 90* on CBS, among other tel-

Alfred Lunt and Lynn Fontanne enjoy a laugh with longtime friend and colleague Noel Coward (c) in the autumn of their lives.
PHOTO BY GLYN LEWIS

evised theater dramas. Also Off-Broadway had come into being and it was making a better go of it than the more sophisticated, classical theater—largely because their operating costs were considerably lower.

This also was the era of mass migration from the city to the suburbs and of the dominance of the automobile. It is no accident that it was often garages that tried to or did in fact replace the old playhouses. Everyone now had a car, and parking in Manhattan has never been plentiful. Meanwhile, NYC urban planner Robert Moses was making efforts for traffic to bypass Manhattan entirely with his expressway right across Greenwich Village. New York City flirted with bankruptcy during the 1970's. By the late '80's the city was back on its feet financially and culturally, but it had been a rocky few decades, especially for high culture in the city. That the Hudson survived at all is, frankly, miraculous. It was, I think, its skill—or luck—at adapting to the times that saved it. The Ron Delsener rock-and-roll era is continuing evidence of that.

15

Ron Delsener Rocks the Hudson: Music Impresario Breathes New Life into the Theater

Music impresario Ron Delsener brought the stars out again on 44th Street. Delsener, who became one of the world's biggest live-event producers in music history, bought the Hudson in 1979 with François de Menil.

Delsener was no stranger to the music business when he bought the Hudson. In 1964 he co-produced the Beatles' first live outdoor concert, not at Shea Stadium, but at the nearby Forest Hills Stadium in Queens, New York. Starting in 1966, his Wolman Ice Skating Rink concert series (in Manhattan's Central Park) featured many big stars. He also produced many Broadway shows including *Bette Midler* at the Palace and Lily Tomlin in *Appearing Nightly* at the Biltmore Theatre.

"It was a 50/50 split with François, $300,000 each," Delsener said of his purchase of the theater. "I had it open for exactly one year. François kept it rented out on a show-by-show basis. I continued to rent the space for one nights—but not many. François took care of it for about two years and then sold the building to Harry Macklowe."

In an interview with the *New York Daily News*, Delsener talked about turning the Hudson into a 1000-seat theater to be reopened as the Savoy nightclub: "When I developed the idea, New York didn't have anything like this. The Bottom Line, the Other End, Brandy's,

Trax, the Village Vanguard, the Village Gate and the rest were offering the audience wooden chairs and incomplete stage facilities. ...

"So I said let's do something soup to nuts," Delsener continued. "Let's do it right. We had to put in a complete fire alarm system, change every door, remove every seat, terrace the orchestra level, resurface all the floors and repaint every square inch of the building. We did all the plumbing, the bars are from Canada, and we're gonna buy ice machines. We bought our own sound and light systems which in this day and age is a little crazy—that's $360,000 right there.

"We thought of everything in the planning of this theater. The ladies' rooms and men's rooms are very, very clean. They're well-appointed and they have attendants. There are drink holders built in behind the theater seats in the loge, and we're having special pink matches made, little things like that. The artists have a suite of dressing rooms backstage. We're building a shower for James Taylor.

"Even the marquee is classy. It's brushed brass lettering, you know, with neon tubes in the letters. At night it's beautiful. In the daytime, you'd think it was on—it's so brilliant, it glows."

"Opening the Savoy is like opening a Broadway show," Delsener said. "There's tremendous pressure because you've invested a million dollars or whatever, and you have to get that money back and it takes many, many years. Talent is a tremendous expense. The profit you make is very small.

"I figure it'll take two, two-and-a-half years to recoup. Of course, there'll always be live entertainment, so I think we're in a good position We just have to get the proper acts. Then again, if we ever left, somebody would walk in and take the place over with no nut. That's the whole key: to go into a place with the least amount of dollars invested."

Delsener may have started the ball rolling but the Hotel Macklowe and later the Millennium Hotel picked it up and ran with it. After the Hudson started use as a venue for special events, in conjunction with the hotel's conference center, businesses often featured bright, modern-day stars in the theater. Gone were Mrs. Fiske, George M. Cohan, and the like. Replacing them were the Pointer Sisters on January 12, 1994, for one business event, followed by one star turn after another. But that story is still a few years away.

Never far from its theater roots, the Hudson became a cabaret in 1992 with an evening of one-act plays. The business manager of the Hudson Theatre Artists Guild persuaded Actors' Equity, the professional actors' union, to agree to let the fledgling company do showcases reserved for 99-seat venues. In other words, only 99 seats of 1,200 seats would be used.

Maybe the Hudson, which started life as a legitimate theater in the "golden age of Broadway," has a way, a life force of its own, resisting all that is not true theater. Delsener tried unsuccessfully to, as one headline said, turn what he renamed the Savoy into a "Pleasure Dome for Grown-up Rockers." But after being dark for several months, a musical called *Manhattan Rhythm*, created by Jon Devlin (who also starred in it), opened with 25 singers, dancers and musicians in a potpourri of a show that included jazz, rock and Latin music. Later that year, the theater planned to showcase Nigerian pop-star King Sunny Ade at an upcoming event shortly after obtaining a liquor license in an effort, according to John Ackerman (Delsener's stage manager), "to make the Hudson financially profitable."

Making money in the pop music biz is not the cakewalk most people think it is. Here's how another top operator, Mr. Sillerman who heads up SFX, sees it. All he wants, Sillerman says, is to be the Sam Walton of pop music, bringing rival promoters—from New York's godfather of gigs, Ron Delsener, to San Francisco's famed Bill Graham Productions—into his big tent. Of course, Wal-Mart is about selling low-cost goods to the masses. SFX, on the other hand, provides high-end, one-stop shopping for the 90-decibel-minstrel set. If you're a touring band, Sillerman wants to book you, market you, promote you, and merchandise you. If you're a fan, he wants to sell you the ticket, the T-shirt, the sixteen-ounce beer. And if you're an advertiser, he wants you to know all those fans are there for the picking. The Savoy/Hudson as a smaller-scale, music-only venue was ultimately unsuccessful.

Developer Harry Macklowe bought the theater and its accompanying air rights in the spring of 1984. *New York Magazine* reported that he agreed to pay owner François de Menil $4.5 million for the Hudson and its air rights which could be transferred to an adjacent tower. Its future on into the next century now seemed assured.

16

Harry Macklowe Buys the Theater and Builds a Hotel

In June 1990 the Hotel Macklowe joined the Hotel Marriott in Times Square's skyward climb that began in the 1980's and continues unabated to this day.

The exterior of the Hudson Theatre had received landmark status in November 1987. The Hotel Macklowe decided to use the theater as a special events venue for its high-tech conference center and renovated the theater and its dressing rooms. One of the first performances, on December 10, 1990, of the reclaimed "legitimate" playhouse was *A Christmas Carol*, starring Jason Robards as Scrooge, the production of which was a benefit for The Actors Fund of America. Tickets were $700 and $100 each.

This gala followed a 24-game world-class chess championship the previous month with Gary Kasparov, then 27, playing Anatoly Karpov with onlookers paying dearly for the privilege.

As more and more corporate events were held in the theater, Macklowe found ways to continue to have it reflect its roots. A so-called "Macklowe Actors Guild" was formed in November 1991. Employees of the hotel, many of whom were also actors, presented a talent showcase open to the public called *It's a Crazy World*. Assistant bell captain Pressley Giles acted as the show's producer and director.

"Macklowe couldn't have razed the landmark building, but everyone would have understood if he had kept it shuttered," Peter Filichia wrote in his "Stagestruck" column in *Theater Weekly* on August 17,

1992. "Corporations used to be that place where your Uncle Sid worked. They were gray monoliths, with elevator banks and long, long fluorescent lit corridors. The kind of place that Billy Wilder made such good sport of in *The Apartment*. But something happened to corporations in the 1980's. They became hip. They started to synergize. They realized that show biz wasn't something to sneer at, but to incorporate into their corporations. Corporate-sponsored events started turning up more and more. I know any number of comedians who owed a great percentage of their incomes to these corporate events during those years. Not surprisingly, the Hudson was stage front and center for this latest show biz trend, the merging of business and show business."

In August 1992, following a multi-million dollar renovation, the interior of the Hudson was officially designated a landmark. And then, for the first time in twenty-seven years, live theater returned to the Hudson. The Hotel Macklowe and the Hudson Theatre Artists Guild co-produced a show called *Beneath the Surface* comprised of three one-act plays. Rock again returned to the Hudson the following year when Meatloaf did a concert. On May 12, 1997, Jeffrey Horowitz, artistic director of the Theater For a New Audience and one of America's very finest producers of Shakespeare, celebrated the Bard's 433rd birthday in a ceremony co-chaired by Aron Feuerstein, president and chief executive of Malden Mills Industries.

The Times Square area, as I've been noting, has certainly experienced its ups and downs during the century-long history of the Hudson. The 1960's and '70's were certainly a shaky period, but even the '80's, a boom era for most of the rest of the city, were still a bit iffy. Roseane Seelan owns the Drama Book Shop on 40th Street between Broadway and Eighth Avenue, an area on the rebound today thanks in part to the new New York Times building at 40th Street and Eighth Avenue. But before this her shop was located on Seventh Avenue in the high 40's in an area that had gone steadily downhill until gentrification began to take hold in earnest in the 1990's. "If we left the shop before 8:00 p.m. it was fine, there were lots of people on the street," she told me. "And again at 10:00 p.m. when the theaters started to let out was also a good time—we could leave. But in the middle it was a wasteland. That was a challenge."

Artist Terence Coyle sketched the Hudson interior (above) in the spring of 2007.

Coyle did this painting of the Helen Hayes Theatre, which started life under Henry B. Harris' management as the Foliés Bergère, and renamed the Fulton and then the Helen Hayes, in the weeks before it was torn down for New York's Marriott Marquis Hotel.

Because of such profound urban evolution, it is perhaps important to remember that these great, old theaters are not guaranteed the long survival that the Hudson has enjoyed. Consider the sad fate of the Hudson's "sister" theater, the Helen Hayes (formerly Henry B. Harris's Fulton Theatre), as chronicled by Terence Coyle, a renowned artist, when the Helen Hayes was razed along with the Morasco Theatre to make room for the Marriott Marquis Hotel.

"Many members of the theatrical community including actors, playwrights, musicians and singers had gathered under the baton of Joe Papp, the famed producer of Shakespeare in the Park, to protest the planned demolition in hopes of saving this and three other theaters," Coyle wrote in *Terence Coyle, A Retrospective at 80*, a book of his work published in connection with a show at the National Arts Club. "With the Helen Hayes Theatre as my motif, I explored the drawing and painting of it from every possible vantage point: from Broadway, from Eighth Avenue ... There was a gaping hole in the east wall through which came the distant sound of Broadway traffic in the otherwise almost spooky and dimmed and vast spaces of the theater."

The theater had opened in 1910 as the Folies Bergère, Broadway's first dinner theater and a more expensive version of the famed Folies Bergère in Paris. A bit of a bust as a dinner theater, it was converted into a conventional Broadway playhouse with traditional raked seating rather than dining tables in the orchestra five months later. Among its most famous tenants were the long-running hit *Abie's Irish Rose* which opened in 1921 but moved to another playhouse, and *Arsenic and Old Lace* which actually moved to the nearby Hudson. Eugene O'Neill's Pulitzer Prize-winning masterpiece, *Long Day's Journey Into Night*, also opened in the theater in 1956.

Coyle told me that seeing the demise of the Helen Hayes, and other playhouses which he painted during the early 1980's, was in a way like witnessing the death of friends.

Without the Herculean efforts of visionary builders like Harry Macklowe and, following him at the Hudson, Chairman Kwek, great city treasures go the way of the poor Helen Hayes Theatre.

17

Chairman Kwek

It was a little like lounging around in one of your fondest, and wildest, dreams. Not too long ago, in real life, I was astonished to find myself sitting in the rounded living room in the Millennium Hotel Paris, looking out at the busy Boulevard Haussman and the pinnacle of the Paris Opera House. Part of me can sense the Germans approaching Paris in the movie fiction of Casablanca; another part of me, Hemingway's *A Moveable Feast*: his views of Paris are the epitome of literature, music, art and just plain life.

Here shortly after writing *Life at the Top: Inside New York's Grand Hotels,* I'm planning another book about hotels and can't help but marvel at Chairman Kwek's far-flung hotel empire, at once modern and sleek, and alternately historic and grand, brimming with the best of the past blending with the best of the present and future. Four months earlier I sat in London with the Chairman (whose full name and business title, by the way, is Kwek Leng Beng, Chairman, Millennium & Copthorne, plc), the owner of this and many other hotels including Broadway's Millennium and its Hudson Theatre.

The Mayfair Millennium is one of several hotels Millennium owns in London. Another of the Chairman's London properties is Bailey's, a traditional and historic hotel built in 1876 which is near Kensington Gardens, Hyde Park and the Natural History Museum. It's right by the Gloucester Hotel in Kensington, which is also a Millennium Hotel.

I sat with Chairman Kwek (referred to by his colleagues as 'the Chairman') one late fall afternoon in the posh restaurant of his

The Hong Leong Group's Executive Chairman, Mr Kwek Leng Beng, was listed as number 185 on Forbes' list of richest people in the world. The Chairman, as he is called by some colleagues and friends, has been a leading champion of restoring historic hotels including The Plaza Hotel in New York, which he co-owned, the Knickerbocker Hotel in Chicago, the Los Angeles Biltmore where the Academy Awards were once held, and the Broadway Millennium's Hudson Theatre. His St. Regis Singapore is scheduled to open on December 20, 2007.

Millennium Knightsbridge Hotel in the heart of London's fashionable Sloane Street shopping district. Our conversation ranged from Gucci, Fendi and other shops in the area to the hotel 'across the pond' in New York City with its Hudson Theatre.

"This hotel was a Holiday Inn a long time ago," he said, referring to the hotel we were in at the moment, as we tasted a special noodle dish. "They had a swimming pool on this level, and then somebody from South Africa took it over. Then during the recession American Express offered me this deal. And I redecorated the lobby and exterior. ..."

The Chairman once took Steve Wynn to the Bombay Brasserie, an Indian restaurant which has made a name for itself as a favorite of celebrities, in the Gloucester. "Was he considering becoming a partner?" I ask. "No, no. He was here, at that time, when London was supposed to be—England was supposed to be—opening up to international casino operators and owners, so he was looking at London, and I happened to be here. I've known him a year. So we talked and I took him to see the Bailey's Hotel. He liked the Bombay Brasserie which he said he could see putting in Las Vegas."

Conversation moved to The New York Plaza Hotel which Chairman Kwek had sold with Prince Alwaleed in 2005. "I know the Prince spoke very highly of you when I talked to him for my Plaza book," I told him. "He said that one of the reasons he got interested in The Plaza in the first place is that you were actually going to run the hotel."

The Chairman replied, "In fact, you know, when he wanted to sell The Plaza, his representative was telling me that he wanted to sell it for about five hundred million, so I thought he wanted to get out. I told him 'I will get out with you together, but leave it to me, I will sell it.' ... So I actually managed to sell for close to seven hundred million.

"What happened was that, you know, the new owner sent his representatives to Singapore to talk with me and then we talked, I think, six hours or so. We agreed on basic terms and just shook hands because it was late and they flew back. And then within a week or so, the owner came over to London so I met up with him. We had lunch in Mayfair, and then we renegotiated. Elad Properties, the company which bought The Plaza, agreed to pay out employee compensation packages for a reduction of $25 million of the $700 million price negotiated thus far.

"The Prince was so happy he invited me to Paris to talk with him so I went to his Georges Cinq. He said that, 'Well, we have known each other now for almost ten years. This is the only project. We mustn't just say goodbye and then we'll continue to forge our relationship for the future—even strengthening it.' I say, 'Sure.' You know, in fact, I have no trouble with the Prince. He's a nice gentleman to work with."

Back in New York I sat down with Paul Underhill, former asset manager of The Plaza and former president of Millennium USA, when he was still president of Millennium. The Plaza had closed its doors as a hotel in 2005. Following a two-year major renovation it will reopen as a combination condominium and hotel.

"The Plaza will finish up having 250 'keys' for the hotel. ... The public areas will stay pretty well as planned. The hotel will be on the 58th Street side and will contain 150 rooms at the moment plus a certain number of condo units which will be sold in conjunction with the hotel. So they finish having 250 keys for the hotel, but they will keep public areas. And at the moment, the ballroom will stay. Of course, they are talking about putting the dome above the Palm Court. The architect, who actually did all of the research at that time on the historical side, had wanted us to put back the dome. It's not going to be the same as it was. Originally it was open to the sky. And after they built the second wing, or addition, on the 58th Street side, they eventually covered it over.

"It is intended a new ceiling will be constructed recreating the original ambience with the aid of lighting. They've got some great ideas and, hopefully, they will come to fruition." As far as the sale of The Plaza is concerned, Underhill said, "if it's a public company that needs to make a profit, it's very difficult to support not selling the hotel."

And now back to London: our talk turned to Singapore and the Chairman's hopes for its artistic accomplishments as well as its business interests. "We are emphasizing now Singapore as a city where you'd like to live, like to work, want also to enjoy yourself," he explained. "That's why we are opening up the casino. The arts have also been a significant feature for the world-class city. Singapore is also an art center. Our Esplanade theater—looks like a porcupine you know—is iconic. So I certainly hope we can do something that is commercially viable. To present the best of Singapore in New York at the Hudson Theatre."

The Chairman and his team are considering a wide variety of options for the Hudson Theatre, he said, including concerts featuring Far Eastern artists and theater productions. "Singapore is promoting arts and culture, so I want to present some of these at the Hudson

Front entrance of the Millennium Hotel today.

Theatre, inviting our best corporate clients, best travel agents," he said. "I know it may not be up to Broadway standards, but at least it's up to a standard that you feel a young country like Singapore can now achieve."

"Our New York hotels are now all doing well. They recently had a food festival, Asian food festival, in the Millennium U.N. Plaza [which, as of this writing, the Chairman has put up for sale]. Our chef from Singapore hotel has won the Chef of the Year in Asia. And our restaurant was Restaurant of the Year. I'm publishing a cookbook for him."

Harry Macklowe's innovativeness in building a state-of-the-art conference center in the hotel, coupled with Chairman Kwek's farsightedness in restoring the Hudson Theatre (which is sometimes used for major conferences as well as gala and theatrical events), has made the Millennium Broadway a powerful magnet for meetings, conventions and theatrical events.

"Basically, Harry did two very innovative things at the theater," explained Paul Underhill, who worked with the hotel and theater over a 13-year period. "One was the 'stepping down' of the seats, rather than traditional raked seating. He also added wonderfully comfortable seats for the theater, which were easily removable for a series of different events. But it took the innovativeness of Chairman Kwek to fully take advantage of that. Not only of the infrastructure but the restoration—bringing the theater back to its former grandeur. You can have a theater production in the evening and the next morning a presentation by a corporation.

"But it was really the Chairman's enthusiasm and support which have brought the Hudson to the wonderful condition it's in today," Underhill concluded.

The renovation and restoration of the Hudson Theatre is very much in keeping with Chairman Kwek's overall vision and philosophy in running his hotel chain. It's essential to emphasize this as he is very mindful of the rich heritage of New York City, Broadway and most importantly, the Hudson Theatre itself. These were all key driving motivations for him in preserving the character of the theater. The Chairman has strong convictions that Broadway is unique to the world. Even though Broadway has undergone many transformations over the years, he believes in the vitality of New York City, in its captains such as former Mayor Giuliani and Mayor Bloomberg, and in the resilience of its people and in the beauty of its location.

After discovering the history of the Hudson Theatre, the Chairman was honored to be the owner of such a historical and important monument. He remains committed to ensuring the Hudson Theatre continues to shine together with the Millennium Hotels. He will continue to preserve the glory of the Hudson Theatre as a reminder of the culture of Broadway and its community. Or, as the Chairman says, "May the glory of the Hudson Theatre continue to flourish in the years to come."

Millennium's historic Knickerbocker Hotel (above left) in Chicago and its Biltmore Hotel in Los Angeles.

Chairman Kwek spends two-thirds of each year in Singapore where he was born and raised and where his Hong Leong Group is now headquartered. The other third of the time he spends playing an active role in the asset management of his vast hotel and other holdings around the globe. He views himself as a real estate developer first and a hotelier second, and learned much about real estate from his late father.

"My father came from China originally," he said. "He started as a building supplier and he went into real estate, not as a developer. His first love was real estate. I took over the chairmanship of Hong Leong Group in 1990, although I had been actively leading several companies within the group before that." (Millennium and Copthorne Hotels plc is a subsidiary of the Hong Leong Group Singapore.)

The Chairman, ever practical, talked about his group of hotels including the historic Biltmore Los Angeles where the Academy Awards ceremonies were once held. "I'm not trying to lead hotel chains. I can't have a critical number like Starwood or Intercontinental; I just can't do that. But I, unlike the hotel people, I have a lot of real estate experience. With the Biltmore Hotel I'm converting some of the offices within the Biltmore, and altogether I'm converting some 200 rooms into condominiums."

Chairman Kwek explained he was a real maverick in the hotel business. "I'm a contrarian in the sense that many hotel companies want to get all the management contracts they can, around the world. My approach to hotels is not only management but real estate. I have an extra strategy. With many of my hotels like the Biltmore we can eventually convert them into condominiums."

"They have another life," I interjected.

"They have another life," he said. "So what we want to do now is seriously look at some of our hotels, to reposition them, bringing some of the hotels to a much higher standard. In fact I have a designer doing a prototype design of the rooms for me in Singapore. The design is 'East Meets West.' It's a fusion between East and West because I strongly believe that, you know, Chinese travel will become the dominant traveling force in years to come. In four or five years, they will be the greatest travelers. And I want them—it's not exactly

Asian design—to feel that they are at home. The luxury of the West, and the touch of the East. ..."

In fact, a number of rooms at the Millennium Biltmore have been designed this way. "The Biltmore, I think, was an 850-room hotel," he said. "The previous owner converted 250 rooms into offices. We're converting back the 250 rooms into condominiums, because downtown Los Angeles now is getting very popular. People living in L.A. have found that, you know, they have to drive for two to three hours every morning, traffic jams, before they can come downtown. So the condominium prices there are very good now. And it is fashionable to have condominiums inside the hotel providing the hotel services to the condominiums. This is quite fashionable now."

New York has long been an international city, catering to all nationalities and tastes, but its hotels have almost always been of a distinctly Western flavor. Will the Chairman's innovations bring about a change in the American businessman and tourist's tastes? Thanks to Millennium Hotels, a slice of the Big Apple has a tantalizing bit of Asian flavoring in the newly renovated rooms of the Millennium Broadway. The hotel's Superior and Classic rooms have been transformed under the expert guidance of SoHo-based architecture and design ateliers, Stonehill & Taylor, one of the country's top design firms.

In keeping with company's hands-on management style, Millennium has remained closely involved with the room design and selection of furnishings, assuring the integrity and caliber of the Asian motifs.

According to Millennium sources, the newly renovated rooms express the "East Meets West" concept, with an emphasis on the simplicity and fluidity of design, as well as the importance of comfort and convenience for the discerning traveler. The updated rooms' new sleek, urban style also conveys the look and feel of a modern home with a generous use of natural colors—intended to induce a calming effect. They also achieve a harmonious balance between the guest and the environment similar to the concept of yin and yang.

New York City is known for its collection of über sophisticated, elegant spaces and the Millennium Broadway's rooms are a welcome addition to this tradition. Some of the rooms feature a chic European-Japanese style platform bed with imported Italian bed linen (sumptuous fabric made from Egyptian cotton with a 440-thread count, which, take their word for it, is very luxe indeed). The simple, straightforward lines of the bed frame, combined with the traditional Asian belief that a bed should be close to the ground, is already in vogue in Europe and is making its way to the United States. The design of the platform bed matches the shape of the dresser, which is modeled from early 19th-century Chinese chests.

The bed's headboard is designed to suggest a classical Chinese partition screen with Chinese cloud motifs etched into the glass section of the headboard. For the convenience of late-night readers, swivel lamps on the left and right are mounted in the headboard. Refined yet subtle features abound such as the Chinese character "fu," which means good luck, imprinted on chair cushions and window sheers as well as Chinese poems woven into the bedspreads.

Stonehill & Taylor also designed the handsome art deco-inspired, oversized yet aerodynamic writing desk. A cozy, art deco-style club chair is located opposite the desk, complemented by an overhead reading light shaped like an 18th century European urn.

Guests are surrounded by "a cloud of peaceful tranquility" courtesy of the Japanese Zen garden-inspired carpet which covers the entire length of the room and nature-themed paintings adjacent to the writing desk and in the bathroom.

These rooms combine not only the best of East and West, but also of Ancient and Supermodern. They provide the latest in technology including a 27" LCD, high-definition, flat-screen TV and Teledex Express Ports for high-speed Internet access.

"The renovated Superior Rooms feature a contemporary cutting-edge feel and look that many will appreciate," explains Per Hellman, general manager for the Millennium Broadway Hotel. "One thing that has not changed is the view! Guests enjoy spectacular views of the city's skyline from most rooms. They also enjoy our matchless location in midtown's Times Square, near Broadway shows, shopping, corporate headquarters and the Javits Center."

Adds Paul Taylor of Stonehill & Taylor: "Our main design concept for the hotel room and the underlying principles behind the Asian-inspired concept is that it should support and enhance the lifestyle of its occupants. The Millennium Broadway is all about comfort, luxury and cosmopolitan style."

The Chairman drove me to his Bailey's Hotel and the Gloucester Hotel, both in London's elegant Kensington district, in his Rolls-Royce. I thought he had a chauffeur. When I got into the back seat, thinking he had a chauffeur, he motioned and told me to sit in the front seat because he was driving.

"When in London, sometimes I stay in my hotel, sometimes I stay in my apartment," the Chairman explained about his own taste in accommodations. "In fact," he said, "when you have a chance, there is another historic hotel called Paris Hotel Millennium Opera. It's a small hotel, 167 rooms, it's not far from the Opera. ..."

And then suddenly my dream, and the interview, was over. I had to relinquish my momentary respite in luxury, say goodbye to the Chairman, and return to the real world.

18

Restoring a Landmark

"There was never any thought of tearing the Hudson down but there was a question of whether to continue to operate it as the ballroom of the hotel," Paul Underhill, former president of Millennium USA, told me. "... You have the permanency, you have the acoustics, the stage, you've got the lighting. To duplicate that in a ballroom is almost impossible. Therefore, to sell it just as a ballroom—you're not selling it. You've got to sell it as a presentation space.

"The other thing that happened is how Times Square over the last ten years evolved. When we were looking at it ten years ago, to think that Toys-R-Us would be our neighbor is something you would have never taken a bit seriously, and that so many of the Fortune 500 companies would relocate and move into offices nearby, and so it became obvious that it had many more things to be used for in addition to functions but those with some theatrical connection.

"At the same time, the Chairman gave his full blessing in the fall of 2004 to maximize the theater ... and, also, for the good of the Times Square district. There was much more demand for various functions in the property. Without the Chairman's blessing it would not have happened. It was not the usual thing you would spend the first money on in the property.

"It became apparent that we were going to look towards doing more than just painting it, and that was to attempt to restore it. For a short-term economic return, you just paint it. It actually started out by our not realizing how much was there which should be treasured! Initially we simply wanted to understand what color the theater was originally painted in. Then they hit something that wasn't plaster; it was glass; we allowed them to cut small pieces out to see what it was!"

Following approval for the project from the New York City Landmarks Preservation Commission, the renovation of the hotel began in earnest under the direction of the renowned architectural design firm, Stonehill & Taylor. Scientific surveys of the theater's structure were conducted before anything else.

Jablonski Berkowitz Conservation, Inc. was then commissioned to tackle the restoration process itself. (Jablonski Berkowitz's impressive portfolio includes the Ellis Island National Historic Site, the Lower East Side Tenement Museum, Radio City Music Hall, and Columbia University's Low Library.) In December 2004, a six-member team began restoring the theater to its original 1903 elegance.

Jablonski Berkowitz first conducted tests under the painted walls and then began to remove paint and plaster from the proscenium arch and cantilevered balcony. While the Millennium Broadway Hotel's management hoped to recover the elegance of turn-of-the-century New York City with the restoration, they got even more than they bargained for.

The surprise came when the Jablonski Berkowitz team uncovered extraordinary Tiffany mosaic tiles around the theater's proscenium arch and decorating the mezzanine and balconies. At some time in the Hudson's past, someone made the odd design decision to paint or plaster over these!

For devotees of Louis Comfort Tiffany it was the 21st-century equivalent of unearthing a lost Egyptian tomb. "The green, pink, turquoise and butterscotch tiles that were uncovered, some only partially intact, were always luxury items," Arlie Sulka, managing director of Lillian Nassau Limited, a Tiffany antiquity dealer, told *Newsday*.

Mary Jablonski expounded a bit about the Tiffany discoveries. "The previous owners who painted and plastered over the precious Tiffany glass artwork had no foresight to the value it brings to the theater. Fortunately, the restoration process will not harm any of these treasures. Much of the distinctive style of the Tiffany artworks are in mint condition and the restoration will only add to the luster of this historical landmark theater."

Some of the tiles had been destroyed when they were covered, in

The cirular stained glass is another example of Louis Comfort Tiffany's artistry

It's hard to believe but these gorgeous Tiffany glass tiles were plastered over in the 1950's in attempt to modernize the Hudson for use at a television studio. Parts of some of the titles were destroyed and restoration artist Angela Caban painted missing patches to blend seamlessly with the originals.

Restoring a Landmark ~ 153

The word 'grand' doesn't really do justice to the Hudson's main entrance hallway. The Belasco Theatre, a few doors from the Hudson, has a very small entrance since the Belasco is not set back from the street. The main part of Hudson Theatre is cl;oser to 45th Street, reached from the theater front entrance on 44th Street via this gilded Peacock Alley-like hallway.

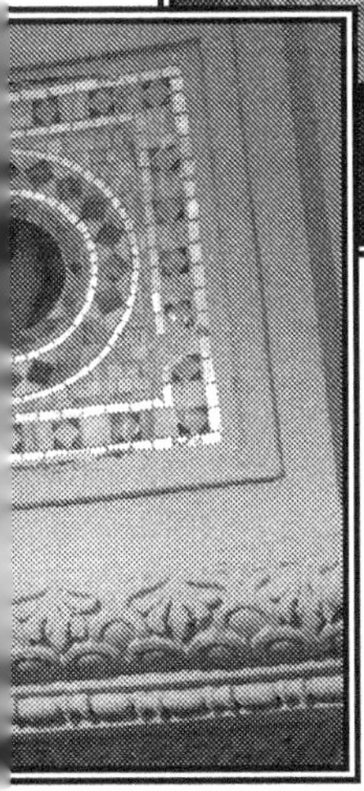

PHOTOS BY ROSE BILLINGS

Actress Angela Caban, who was in the cast of Andrew Lloyd Webber's musical "Cats" for some years, exchanged her dancing shoes for paint brushes in helping restore interior of the Hudson.

the 1950's when the Broadway house was employed as a TV studio. Not to worry, all of them were lovingly brought back to their opening night appearance circa 1903. It required very costly, very tedious work, often employing dental equipment, to restore the Tiffany glass.

Angela Caban, a decorative painter, restoration artist and owner of the Finished Wall, has worked on some significant New York City apartments. She spent days and weeks lying face up on elevated platforms supported by scaffolding. Hers was painstaking work—often requiring use of a brush that looked more like a few strands of hair than a customary multi-bristle brush to get the colors just right. In some cases she had to recreate glass "tiles" that were missing by painting sections to look like the missing tiles. Now, even close up, it all remains remarkably realistic.

Angela Caban was also an actress in the company of *Cats* for several years. She took special pride in her part in helping to restore the interior of the Hudson because Mrs. Fiske was a distant relative. (As mentioned previously Mrs. Fiske was a big theater star from the late 1890's through the early 1930's.)

I caught up with her on her cell phone as she was driving down to Charleston. "Every couple of weeks I just pop into the theater when I'm in the area," Ms. Caban explained, the traffic roaring around her. "To me, it is a sacred space. The theater is like a church and I feel so happy to have been a part of the restoration process."

How did she start in this biz? "I used to draw quite a bit when I was younger. I was always kind of arts-and-crafts orientated but it wasn't until I was in *Cats* that I would come home—I covered six roles in that show—some nights just a little stressed out and to calm down what I would do is I would paint my apartment and I would try different finishes. And then I would do other performers' apartments and that's when I went back to school to get my degree in fine art."

The Hudson Theatre had already had a distinguished association with Tiffany, the world-famous designer of distinctive glass and other objects (most famously his Tiffany lamps). Today the theater is spectacularly replete with Tiffany ceilings and chandeliers, all of which have been gloriously restored to original condition.

In addition to the restoration work on the Tiffany glass pieces, the lobby, foyer and the stage's proscenium arch were repainted to replicate the original color schemes of the Hudson Theatre. Boxes were gilded once again in gold. Stonehill & Taylor brought their interior design expertise to the renovations of the theater, providing exclusively made new furnishings and finishes to enhance the vibrancy of the Tiffany mosaics and gilding. Custom designed carpeting was laid down and new authentic stage curtains put up. One of the unique features of the Hudson is the removable handrails in the seating area which allows for flexible seating arrangements in accordance to the specifications of different events. Lighting and sound engineers were brought in to make certain that re-wired crystal chandeliers, lighting upgrades and the sound/lighting control systems met Millennium's high hotel standards.

"This theater is one of the most significant pieces of architecture in New York City and we are definitely looking forward to the restoration of the theater's facilities as well as enjoying the newly discovered Tiffany artwork,"

Per Hellman, vice president and general manager of the Millennum Broadway Hotel, spent many years managing The Waldorf-Astoria. On December 10, 2005, he received the Theatre Museum Award on behalf of the Broadway Millennium in honor of its excellence in Theatre History Preservation in restoring the Hudson.

explained Per Hellman, when he was vice-president and general manager for the Millennium Broadway Hotel. "What is even more exciting is that groups can actually rent out this space and feel like they are a part of history!"

The Hudson Theatre restoration took nearly eight months and more than $1.2 million to complete but it was eventually finished by the summer of 2005. The Millennium Broadway's Hudson Theatre restoration has been one of the most exciting projects undertaken during the rejuvenation of the historic Times Square/Broadway district of New York City. Needless to say, this is an area that has witnessed big changes over the years. One aspect that has not changed, however, is the district's love affair with glamour and celebrity.

Well, it was a long, long time coming, but that grand old lady of the New York theater has finally received her sparkling new dress.

Sudheer Ragavan, formerly a top executive of Singapore Airlines, is also the former president of Millennium USA. Ragavan believes the Hudson will continue to have life as a theater as well as a corporate meeting venue. While the hotel is one of the best in Times Square and, for that matter, New York, he saw another side of life as a child.

"When I was born [in Singapore] we were living above a shop and we had a room. See that flower?" He pointed to a flowering plant in Charlotte's Restaurant in the Millennium Hotel. "From about there to about here [maybe 25 feet] and that was our living space. Most people were poor. And in this space we had our living arrangement and my mother had a little place to cook. There was a communal toilet. I've seen Singapore change to where I live today where each of my children has its own room with its own toilet. That was my origin and there were many of my generation who have come this far. We've seen the transformation of not just the people but also the island. But it doesn't have the history. We are the history. And it's fantastic coming to a place like this where there is so much modernity and at the same time you just scratch the surface and there is such deep history."

He worked for Singapore Airlines before being named president of Millennium Hotels. "When I finished I was running sales and marketing for Singapore Airlines Cargo, but I've done my stints from the lowest ranks up to 'country manager' in various places. ... I ran the biggest sales unit we have which is in Singapore and then I went to do

Called the Queens Box, these box seats, located on the right and left of the Hudson's proscenium arch, appear to be mini-stages from a distance.

revenue management and worked up to do sales and marketing cargo. And decided I will take a break and join another industry.

"Both airline seats and hotel rooms are perishable products. The fundamental principles are the same. They are perishable so you have to sell them today. If you don't, well, you cannot keep it for the next day, number one. Number two, you can sell a unit of the product anytime before it is consumed. The same unit of the product can be consumed by people from various market segments. Pay a different price for the same unit of product. There's a romance about both and that's what I'm trying to capture, get my people to capture here."

Per Hellman, former vice president and general manager of The Waldorf-Astoria Hotel, is now general manager of the 1500-room Broadway Millennium and its adjacent luxury Premier Tower, with a separate entrance and slightly bigger rooms.

The Premier is situated immediately to the east of the Hudson Theatre—between it and what used to be called the Girard Hotel, where the popular French bistro *Un, Deux, Trois* is located today. It generally has more spacious rooms and a separate check-in area. It is, in its own modest way, akin to the Waldorf Towers as the more luxurious upper floors of The Waldorf-Astoria Hotel are called.

"It absolutely astounds me knowing the value, not only the monetary value, but the antique value," Mr. Hellmann said about the Hudson Theatre. "Not only the investor value but the antique value of the Tiffany glass back in the early 1900's. He [Henry B. Harris] apparently got the design scheme on a trip to Turkey."

Chairman Kwek actually wooed Hellman out of retirement after he left The Waldorf-Astoria, first to manage the Millenium Hilton opposite the World Trade Center site then the Millennium Mayfair in London and then the Millennium Broadway.

Michael Littler, former general manager of the Millennium Broadway Hotel, started working at the hotel in 1993 at a time when the Times Square area was widely considered as unsafe as it was seedy. He even arranged for guests at the hotel to be escorted to subway stops and theaters to ensure their well-being. But he became so fascinated with the 44th Street block and the area in general, he wrote a book about it. Called *A Highly Personalized Guide to the Immediate Neighborhood*, it takes readers on a tour of the neighborhood, rich in theatrical lore and history. Here's a sample: "Located in the Gerard Hotel is the *Café Un Deux Trois*, a well-known restaurant in the area. The Gerard is now rental apartments. [The hotel] was opened in 1894 as a moderate hotel catering to respectable people, according to its owners. I thought that was quaint and very interesting; just what was their mission?" Stopping at the Belasco Theatre, Littler wrote, "It is the sixth oldest theater on Broadway. Founder David Belasco ... was also among the first to exploit the new medium of the electric light to create stunningly realistic effects. He also helped found the Ashcan School of Art which focused on realistic depictions of street life for a publication called *The Masses*."

19

Looking to the Future, Theatre Museum, Plans

So once again, in honoring its heritage—the heritage of Broadway generally—the Hudson Theatre has carved out a unique position for itself for future generations.

"Thank you all for coming tonight, coming to support the Theatre Museum," said Tony Award-winning Broadway producer Stewart F. Lane, chairman of The Broadway Trustees of the Theatre Museum, to those who were gathered at the Hudson for the 2006 Theatre Museum Awards. "It's with your support that we are able to announce tonight that at our offices here on Broadway we will have our first exhibit open to the public by appointment only. It will be of the theaters on Broadway and their history, including a 10-or 15-minute videotape explaining what we do as a museum and the history of the theaters, and then we take them on a tour of the office where the pictures of the theaters will be exhibited."

Fred Papert, who created the 42nd Street Development Corporation in 1976 to revive the western fringes of 42nd Street, received the Theatre Museum's History Preservation Award. The group transformed dilapidated old buildings—true eyesores—into Off-Broadway theaters. A rebuilt Theatre Row now contains five theaters, six rehearsal rooms, office spaces and a café.

Papert, in accepting the award, said he was "particularly pleased to be on a bill with such theater giants as the Manhattan Theatre Club ... and, of course, Helen Guditis, whose cause is worthy and wonderful.

[Guditis is president of the Theatre Museum.] Thirty-something years ago, another giant in the theater world, Bob Moss, moved Playwrights Horizons into an awfully seedy set of offices in a building on 42nd Street between Ninth and Tenth Avenues. And one day Bob looked out his window and saw someone out in the street in a suit and a tie. And it was me! And I said we're buying these buildings and starting a renewal over here, and he said, 'What are you doing with the buildings?' I said, 'All we know is we want them to anchor a renewal in this part of town.' And he said, 'Build theaters.' And that's why Theatre Row got built. So when I stand here getting glimmers of credit for being in the theater business, I feel a little strange about it.

"On the other hand, let me offer some slight theater bona-fides. I want you to know that I have two aunts who were in the Ziegfeld Follies ... and forty blocks south in *Greenwich Village Follies*, a very elegant 'stage door Johnny' of 42 or 43 years old met a 17-year-old dancer in the Greenwich Village Follies, married her, and I am the second child of that marriage ... and on my mother's side, sure there were serious actors. So I'm not sure why we are being honored in this prestigious group of theater people—and we're not giving the reward back under any circumstances!"

The Manhattan Theatre Club's restoration of the Biltmore Theatre, Lundeana M. Thomas of the African-American Theatre Program at the University of Louisville, and the Drama League Directors Project were also honored at the Hudson Theatre.

"In theater," Helen Guditis told me over tea at the Algonquin Hotel, that venerable inn to the east of the Hudson, "it is always important to make sure that the bread-and-butter issues are taken care of." The fact that the Hudson Theatre itself is not dependent on theatrical productions is wonderful and that means the theater can have a kind of never-ending life.

In fact, Guditis marvels that the Hudson has "a day job," being used for corporate events during the daylight hours. "It's very attractive to people in the corporate world who use that space and, whether they know it or not, they are being seduced with very interesting architecture—and perhaps even some theater ghosts. They might even go to the theater!"

But the Hudson is not her favorite theater. "I have to say, I love the

Lyceum Theatre. I have kind of an affinity for the Lyceum," she said. "I think when some people just walk into a place it kind of sits right with them. And you don't know why. It could be a number of reasons."

In the early fall of 2005, Guditis talked about the upcoming Theatre Museum gala held at the Hudson Theatre. "It's going to be October 10, on Monday from 6 to 9. And in the tradition of the Broadway Theater Institute, the Broadway Museum is honoring unsung heroes in two arenas. One is theater productions. The other is theater arts education. For the theater custom preservation prospective we're looking at honoring 10 Chimneys Foundation. 10 Chimneys is the historic summer house of Alfred Lunt and Lynn Fontanne. It was saved from the wrecking ball and was brought back to its former glory. And it literally was the summer camp of the Broadway world of their time. From the 1920's to the 1980's. ... They have also created a learning center. They are now a major repository for theater history. They are actually going to be featured on *CBS This Morning* on September 25 just before our awards ceremony."

Guditis notes, "The theater that I am so delighted they brought back is the New Amsterdam Theatre." While the Hudson has had a longer and much more varied life as a theater, few if any of the historic Broadway playhouses can compete with the New Amsterdam for sheer beauty. Guditis remembers seeing the renovated and reconstructed New Amsterdam for the first time. "At the opening of each musical they have what they call a Gypsy Robe ceremony. On the opening night of *The Lion King* at the New Amsterdam, I got there a little bit early. And somehow or another, I ended up walking out on stage and being the only one on that stage and looking out into this newly renovated theater and it was just an awe-inspiring moment."

Guditis, who "started doing plays in kindergarten," trained professionally as an actor. She went to the American Academy of Dramatic Arts and received a Masters Degree in theater. She was, however, shocked at how hard it was to stay in the "business" of acting and started to do theater "to help individuals to develop, so I got interested in doing acting education work."

"I loved doing a show. I loved creating a part, but in order to succeed in the business you have to be driven. You have to be focused and driven. I really wanted a whole life."

Looking to the Future, Theatre Museum, Plans ～ 163

Photos by Rose Billings

Tony Award-winning actresses Jane Alexander and Morain Seldes joined former New York City Mayor David Dinkins at the Hudson Theatre in May 2007 for a gala 85th birthday tribute for Wynn Handman, co-founder of Off-Broadway's stellar American Place Theatre.

Broadway and cabaret superstar Barbara Cook (left) joined Joanne Woodward, Marian Seldes, Jane Alexander and others on stage at the Hudson in paying tribute to American Place Theatre co-founder Wynn Handman.

The history of the Hudson, which to no small extent incorporates the history of the Broadway theater in general, has had many such awe-inspiring moments. It is producers and newspapermen decrying plans to tear down the theater. It is George M. Cohan going into his crazy dance. It is Steve Allen and Elvis and Jack Paar. It's not so much the Theatre Museum looking back, honoring the glory days of Broadway; it's looking to the future, always looking to the future in an endless cycle of adventure and color and comedy and drama.

One nearby Broadway institution that has both a glorious past and

William Wolf, President of drama Deck, a society of theater writers, is former film critic for the Garrett newspaper chain and a contributing editor of New York Magazine. He is editor of the website "New York Calling". He is at the Hudson with his wife, Lillian Kramer Wolf, co-author with Willam Wolf of "The Cinema and Our Century". PHOTO BY ROSE BILLINGS

Joanne Woodward, a longtime supporter of Off-Broadway's American Place Theatre, is pictured here with American Place co-founder and director Wynn Handman who celebrated his 85th birthday at the Hudson Theatre. The American Place, co-founded by Handman in 1963, was one of the first off-Broadway theaters to locate in the Times Square area. Over the years, it produced eight plays by Sam Shepard. PHOTO BY ROSE BILLINGS

still rosy future is the venerable Sardi's Restaurant. With hundreds of Alex Gard caricatures decorating its walls, the famous bistro opened at its current location at 234 West 44th Street in March 1927. It remains a thriving Times Square institution still frequented by Broadway and Hollywood luminaries even though it has much greater competition than ever these days as new restaurants have opened by the score. Columnist Walter Winchell and my father added to its popularity in the early years by forming the Cheese Club, where newspaper scribes would gather much like the more famous Algonquin Round Table at the Algonquin Hotel down the street from the Hudson.

20

Epilogue

Today, celebrities from the world of theater and movies stand in awe of the Hudson's restoration. "It's a fantastic theater," two-time Tony nominee Alan Rickman told me at a gala for the Only Make Believe charity in November 2006 held at the Hudson. "It should be a theater again! It's a beautiful, beautiful theater."

David Bryan, who has been with Bon Jovi for many years, performed at the gala. "It's my first time working here," he said. He did not remember the Hudson when it was the Savoy Nightclub. "In the '80's we didn't play too many clubs around here. We got signed and just went on tour. But we were one of the first acts when the Nokia Theatre [just west of the Hudson] opened as a rock venue." Former talk show host Kathie Lee Gifford, as one of the charity's biggest supporters, introduced the night's talent line-ups. One of the stars was Donny Osmond who was starring in Disney's *Beauty and the Beast* at the nearby Lunt-Fontanne Theatre on Broadway.

"It's interesting I'm doing a Disney show," Osmond told the audience from the same stage where George M. Cohan and Ethel Barrymore once played. "If you go way back it was Walt Disney himself who discovered my brothers. It's because of the Disney organization that I'm in this business."

To this latter comment, Kathie Lee rejoined with a big smile, "which makes you like an indentured slave!"

One hundred and three years had passed since the Hudson opened. Barrymore, Cohan, Harris, Hart, Lunt, Paar, Presley, Allen, Woollcott. The great and near-great have made the Hudson their the-

American playwright Sam Shepard and film and stage star Jessica Lange joined dozens of celebrities honoring Wynn Handman on an 85th birthday bash at the Hudson Theatre in May, 2007 PHOTO BY ROSE BILLINGS

Andra McDonald, Tony Award-winning Broadway star, with Donald Billings (left) and Robert Blume, a producer of The Drama Desk Awards. PHOTO BY ROSE BILLINGS

Making her stage debut in 1955 at the New York City Center, run by the late Jean Dalrymple, Doris Roberts, really didn't become a star until she was cast as Ray Romano's mom in the mega-hit TV series "Everybody Loves Raymond." Here she pays tribute to longtime friend and colleague Wynn Handman at the Hudson Theatre. PHOTO BY ROSE BILLINGS

ater home. It has survived them all, a beam of light for the next hundred years when the beloved brainchild of Henry B. Harris will still light up the sky of 44th Street at the Crossroads of the World.

What is it that great Oscar Hammerstein lyric tells us from his masterpiece *Show Boat*? "That ole man river, he just keeps on rollin' along." The Hudson Theatre, like that great river not too far from its doors to the west, just seems to keep rolling along—sometimes rolling with the punches, sometimes rock and rolling, sometimes rolling out the red carpet—but it keeps on rolling nonetheless, and America is the richer for it.

APPENDICES

Ethel Barrymore, George M. Cohan, Elvis and hundreds of other stars have graced the stage of the Hudson.

APPENDIX A
Findings and Designations

On the basis of a careful consideration of the history, the architecture and other features of this Interior, the Landmarks Preservation Commission finds that the Hudson Theatre, first floor interior consisting of the ticket lobby, the inner lobby, the auditorium, the stage, the staircases leading from the first floor of the orchestra to the first balcony floor; the first balcony floor interior consisting of the first balcony, the upper part of the auditorium; the second balcony floor interior consisting of the second balcony, the upper part of the auditorium and ceiling; and the fixtures and interior components of these spaces, including but not limited to, wall and ceiling surfaces, doors, stair railings and attached decorative elements; has a special character, special historical and aesthetic interest and value as part of the development, heritage and cultural characteristics of New York City, New York State, and the nation, and the Interior or parts thereof are thirty years old or more, and that the Interior is one which is customarily open and accessible to the public, and to which the public is customarily invited.

The Commission further finds that, among its important qualities, the Hudson Theatre Interior survives today as one of the historic theater interiors that symbolize American theater for both New York and the nation; that, built in 1902-04, it is among the oldest legitimate theaters surviving in New York City; that it was part of a turn-of-the-century burst of theater construction that helped shape the character of the newly emerging theater district around Times Square; that it was designed to house the stars, productions, and offices of Henry B. Harris, a top Broadway producer of the era, and as such represents a special aspect of the nation's theatrical history; that the interior, begun by J. B. McElfatrick & Son and completed by Israels & Harder, is an unusually handsome neo-classical design; that the architecturally significant features in its auditorium and lobby spaces include Tiffany glass domes, elegant plasterwork ornamentation, and unusual light-fixtures; that for three quarters of a century the Hudson Theatre Interior has served as home to countless numbers of the plays through which the Broadway theater has come to personify American theater; and that as such it continues to help define the Broadway theater district, the largest and most famous concentration of legitimate stage theaters in the world.

Accordingly, pursuant to the provisions of Chapter 21, Section 534, of the Charter of the City of New York and Chapter 8-A of the Administrative Code of the City of New York, the Landmarks Preservation Commission designates as an Interior Landmark the Hudson Theatre, first floor interior consisting of the ticket lobby, the inner lobby, the auditorium, the stage, the staircases leading from the first floor of the orchestra to the first balcony floor; the first balcony floor interior consisting of the first balcony, the upper part of the auditorium; the second balcony floor interior consisting of the second balcony, the upper part of the auditorium and ceiling; and the fixtures and interior components of these spaces, including but not limited to, wall and ceiling surfaces, doors, stair railings, and attached decorative elements; 139-141 West 44th Street, Borough of Manhattan and designates Tax Map Block 997, Lot 15, Borough of Manhattan, as its Landmark Site.

APPENDIX B

Designation by the Landmarks Preservation Commission of the Hudson as an Official Landmark

DESCRIPTION 1

TICKET LOBBY:

The ticket lobby is a square space with two ticket windows and a staircase on the east wall. On the north wall, leading from the vestibule, are doors set below transoms; doors opening into the main lobby are on the north wall. The ceiling rises from a shallow cove.

1) **Ornament:** Decorative ornament includes but is not limited to the following:

Walls: The walls, lined with gold-veined dark green marble, terminate in a shallow cornice. Caryatids flanking the ticket windows support an entablature. Above the marble is a wide plasterwork band adorned with neo-classical foliation.

Ceiling: Classical moldings line the ceiling cove, setting off the main portion of the plasterwork ceiling, composed of bands surrounding the closely spaced coffers adorned with foliate decoration enclosing light sockets.

2) **Attached Fixtures:**

Transoms: The transoms above the entrance doors are filled with leaded glass.
Ticket Windows: The ticket windows have bronze frames with coffered bands at the top.

Light fixtures: The candelabra-type chandeliers have crystal pendants.

INNER LOBBY:

The inner lobby is a long rectangular space with doors at the south end leading from the ticket lobby and a doorway to the auditorium on the north end.

1) **Ornament:** Decorative ornament includes but is not limited to the following:

Walls: The plasterwork walls are articulated by paneled Ionic pilasters flanking arches (now filled in with mirrors), above a paneled wainscoting. The arch spandrels are adorned with foliation. One arch opens to a stairhall. The pilasters support a decorative foliate cornice just below the ceiling.

Ceiling: The plasterwork ceiling contains three stained-glass domes (see below under attached fixtures) and is divided into sections by wide bands decorated with classical ornament. Small stained-glass panels (see below under attached fixtures) are placed at the edges of the ceiling and surrounded by decorative bands.

2) **Attached Fixtures:**

Lighting fixtures: A candelabra-type chandelier with crystal pendants is suspended from the center dome. Shallow crystal light fixtures surround the domes.

Stained Glass: There are three oval stained-glass domes in the ceiling. Stained-glass panels are placed along the edge of the ceiling.

AUDITORIUM:

1) Configuration: The configuration of the auditorium consists of a space which is slightly wider than it is deep with two balconies, a

proscenium flanked by boxes, a sounding board, an orchestra promenade, balcony promenades, a ceiling, and a stage opening behind the proscenium arch.

Proscenium: The proscenium is a depressed arch.
Sounding board: A sounding board rises from the proscenium arch and above the boxes.
Balconies: There are two balconies.
Boxes: Boxes are located at the level of the first balcony and have curved fronts.
Ceiling: The ceiling rises from groined sections and is flat.
Staircases: A staircase rises from the orchestra promenade to the first balcony.
Stage: The stage extends behind the proscenium arch and forms a stage picture (visible from the audience) framed by the proscenium arch.2
Promenades: Promenades are located at the rear of the orchestra and both balconies.

2) **Ornament:**

The decorative ornament is plasterwork in relief, which is integrated into the surfaces which define the configuration of the auditorium. Decorative ornament includes, but is not limited to, the following:

Proscenium arch: The proscenium arch is composed of a wide paneled band with Greek key motifs encompassing light sockets and square panels with iridescent glazed terra-cotta insets (now all painted except one). The entire band is flanked by laurel leaf moldings.
Sounding board: The sounding board is outlined by foliate bands and moldings, which create a cove, and is covered with hexagonal panels with center light sockets.
Orchestra: The side walls have paneled pilasters.
Orchestra promenade: The rear wall is paneled. The ceiling above the promenade is divided into paneled sections by bands and moldings.
Boxes: Each box with a curved front is flanked by paired fluted

columns and pilasters with Corinthian capitals. These support an entablature with a foliate frieze, dentilled cornice, and cresting.

Balconies: The side walls of both balconies have paneled pilasters. The undersides of the balconies are adorned with foliate bands. Columns with foliate capitals support the the <sic> second balcony. The balcony fronts are paneled and outlined by moldings.

Ceiling: Wide bands with moldings and octagonal panels rise from the side walls of the second balcony, creating groined panels. These panels are adorned with neoclassical foliation surrounding fixtures. Banks and moldings articulate the ceiling. A highly ornate foliate panel is at the rear above the second balcony.

3) ***Attached fixtures:***

Staircases: The staircase in the orchestra promenade has a decorative wrought-iron railing.

Light fixtures: The ceiling lighting is original, consisting of glazed bulbs hung with crystal pendants. Bulbs without pendants are in the rear panel above the second balcony. Rows of bulbs are placed in the coves outlining the sounding board. Existing non-original light fixtures on the underside of the balconies are stylistically compatible with the interior.

Standing rails: Paneled standing rails separate the balcony promenades from the balcony seats.

Known alterations:

The rake of the orchestra floor has been removed. The columns and standing rail in the orchestra promenade have been covered over with modern materials. Modern technical booths have been installed at the rear of both balconies. A modern enclosed lighting box has been installed on the front of the second balcony. Many original light sockets for bulbs remain, but are no longer in use (see above). The current color scheme obscures the effect of the decorative ornament.

(MP)

Notes

1. This description identifies the spaces that are included in this designation. Specific elements are listed, and architecturally significant features are underlined as explained in the "Guidelines for Treatment of Theater Interiors" as adopted by the Landmarks Preservation Commission on December 10, 1985.

2. For the purposes of this description, the stage shall include the enclosing walls and roof of the stage house and a floor area behind the proscenium arch, but not any fixture or feature of or within that space.

Conclusion

The Hudson Theatre Interior survives today as one of the historic theater interiors that symbolize American theater for both New York and the nation. One of the first group of theaters to be constructed in the newly emerging Times Square area, it helped shape the character of the theater district. Today it survives as one of the oldest legitimate Broadway theaters. Built for Henry B. Harris, the Hudson served as home for his productions and his stars. The elegant interior by Israels & Harder, recognized in its day as an unusually handsome design, represents an important aspect of the nation's theatrical history.

APPENDIX C
Productions at the Hudson

1903

Cousin Kate — a comedy by Hubert Henry Davies
Produced by: Charles Frohman
Cast included: Ethel Barrymore and Bruce McRae
Opened: October 19, 1903 (44 perfs.)

The Marriage of Kitty — by Cosmo Gordon-Lennox from the French of "La Passerelle" by Fred de Gresac and François de Croisset
Produced by: Charles Frohman
Cast included: Marie Tempest, Leonard Boyne, Ada Ferrar and Gilbert Hare
Opened: November 30, 1903 (51 perfs.)

1904

The 1904/1905 season brought about one of the most remembered roles of this time. In the production of *Sunday*, Ethel Barrymore utters one of the all-time classic lines of her career: "That's all there is, there isn't anymore."

Plays Presented at the Hudson this Year:

Ranson's Folly — by Richard Harding Davis
Produced by: Robert Edeson
Cast included: Robert Edeson
Opened: January 18, 1904 (61 perfs.)

Man Proposes — a comedy by Ernest Denny
Produced by: Charles Frohman
Cast included: Henry Miller and Margaret Anglin
Opened: March 11, 1904 (24 perfs.)

Cousin Kate — a comedy by Hubert Henry Davies
Produced by: Charles Frohman
Cast included: Ethel Barrymore and Bruce McRae
Opened: April 4, 1904 (16 perfs.)
NB. This was a return engagement.

Camille — by Alexandre Dumas Jr.
Produced by: Charles Frohman
Cast included: Margaret Anglin, Henry Miller and Bruce McRae
Opened: April 18, 1904 (16 perfs.)

Letty — by Arthur Wing Pinero
Produced by: Charles Frohman
Cast included: William Favrsham
Opened: September 12, 1904 (64 perfs.)

Sunday — by Thomas Raceward
Produced by: Charles Frohman
Cast included: Ethel Barrymore, Bruce McRae and Edgar Selwyn
Opened: November 15, 1904 (79 perfs.)

1905

The Hudson Theatre presented an abridged version of George Bernard Shaw's *Man and Superman*. This was the first time Shaw allowed a version of one of his plays that he had not written himself to be shown. This is also the year Henry B. Harris opened one of his most successful plays, *The Lion and the Mouse.* at the Lyceum, The play's success was so grand that during one season four road companies were presenting the play simultaneously.

Plays Presented at the Hudson this Year:

Strongheart — by William C. DeMille
Produced by: Robert Edeson
Directed by: William Harris and Taylor Holmes
Cast included: Robert Edeson, Macey Harlan and Richard Sterling
Opened: January 30, 1905 (66 perfs.)

NB. William C. DeMille (1878-1955) was an elder brother of Cecil B. DeMille (1881-1959)

The Hour-Glass — by William Butler Yeats
Cathleen Ni Houlihan — by William Butler Yeats
The Land of Heart's Desire — by William Butler Yeats
Produced by: Margaret Wycherly
Opened: February 21, 1905 (1 perf.)
NB. This production comprised three one-act plays.

The Lady Shore — by Mrs. Vance Thompson and Lena R. Smith
Produced by: Virginia Harned
Cast included: Virginia Harned and Robert Loraine
Opened: March 27, 1905 (16 perfs.)

A Blot in the 'Scutcheon — by Robert Browning
Produced by: Mrs. Sarah Cowell Le Moyne
Cast included: Mrs. Sarah Cowell Le Moyne and Grace Elliston
Opened: April 7, 1905 (5 perfs.)

The Heir to the Hoorah — by Paul Armstrong
Produced by: Kirke La Shelle
Cast included: Guy Bates Post and Beverly Sitgreaves
Opened: April 10, 1905 (59 perfs.)

Man and Superman — by George Bernard Shaw
Produced by: Charles Dillingham
Cast included: Richard Bennett, Fay Davis and Clara Bloodgood
Opened: September 5, 1905 (192 perfs.)

1906

Henry B. Harris purchased the Hackett Theatre for a reported $400,000 this year. Originally the Lew M. Fields Theatre, the Hackett was built by Oscar Hammerstein in 1904 at 254 West 42nd Street. Henry's younger brother, William Jr., managed the theater which, in 1911, was renamed the Harris in honor of Henry's father, William Sr.

Plays Presented at the Hudson this Year:

The Duel — translated by Louis N. Parker from the French of
  Henri Lavedan
Produced by: Charles Frohman
Cast included: Otis Skinner and Guy Standing
Opened: February 12, 1906 (73 perfs.)

The American Lord — by Charles T. Dazey and
George H. Broadhurst
Produced by: Charles Frohman
Cast included: William H. Crane, Elmer Grandin and Edgar Norton
Opened: April 16, 1906 (32 perfs.)

The Hypocrites — by Henry Arthur Jones
Produced by: Charles Frohman
Cast included: Richard Bennett, Jessie Millward and Doris Keane
Opened: August 30, 1906 (209 perfs.)

1907

Brewster's Millions — by Winchell Smith and Byron Ongley
  from the novel by George Barr McCutcheon
Produced by: Frederic Thompson and Winchell Smith
Directed by: Frederic Thompson and Winchell Smith
Cast included: Jack Devereaux and Edward Abeles
Opened: New Amsterdam/December 31, 1906
then Hudson/February 25, 1907 (163 perfs.)

The Lion and the Mouse — by Charles Klein
Produced by: Henry B. Harris
Directed by: William Harris and R. A. Roberts
Cast included: Richard Bennett, Edmund Breese and Grace Elliston
Opened: Lyceum/November 20, 1905; Grand Opera House/May
  27, 1907; Hudson/June 17, 1907; and Academy of Music/October
  28, 1907 (586 perfs.)

Classmates — an American play by William C. DeMille

and Margaret Turnbull
Produced by: George W. Barnum
Directed by: George W. Barnum
Cast included: Robert Edeson and George W. Barnum
Opened: August 29, 1907 (102 perfs.)

The Chorus Lady — a comedy by James Forbes
Produced by: James Forbes
Staged by: James Forbes
Cast included: Rose Stahl and Francis Byrne
Opened: November 25, 1907 (33 perfs.)

Her Sister — by Clyde Fitch and Cosmo Gordon-Lennox
Produced by: Clyde Fitch
Cast included: Ethel Barrymore and Lucile Watson
Opened: December 25, 1907 (61 perfs.)

1908

Henry B. Harris bought bought out George C. Heye's share in the Hudson Theatre for approximately $700,000. Harris became the sole holder of the property's title on April 1, 1908.

Plays Presented at the Hudson this Year:

The Honor of the Family — by Paul M. Potter from the French of Émile Fabre adapted from the novel "La Rabouilleuse" by Honoré de Balzac
Produced by: Gustav Von Seyffertitz
Cast included: Otis Skinner, Albert G. Andrews and Walter F. Scott
Opened: February 17, 1908 (104 perfs.)

Love's Comedy — by Henrik Ibsen
Produced by: George Ford
Opened: March 23, 1908

The Call of the North — by George H. Broadhurst
Produced by: Robert Edeson

Directed by: Robert Edeson
Cast included: Robert Edeson, Macey Harlan, David Torrence and Marjorie Wood
Opened: August 24, 1908 (32 perfs.)

The Offenders — by Elmer Blaney Harris
Produced by: Maurice Campbell
Cast included: Robert Edeson, John Flood and Katherine Grey
Opened: September 23, 1908 (22 perfs.)

Pierre of the Plains — by Edgar Selwyn based on the book series "Pierre and His People" by Sir Gilbert Parker
Produced by: Edgar Selwyn
Cast included: Elsie Ferguson, Edgar Selwyn, Joseph Adelman and George Schaeffer
Opened: October 12, 1908 (32 perfs.)

Lady Frederick — a comedy by W. Somerset Maugham
Produced by: William Seymour
Staged by: William Seymour
Cast included: Ethel Barrymore and Bruce McRae
Opened: November 9, 1908 (96 perfs.)

1909
Plays Presented at the Hudson this Year:

The Third Degree — by Charles Klein
Produced by: Charles Klein
Directed by: Charles Klein
Cast included: Wallace Eddinger and George Barnum
Opened: February 1, 1909 (168 perfs.)

Disengaged — a comedy by Henry James
Directed by: Fritz Williams
Cast included: Louise Closser Hale, Dorothy Donnelly, Frank Gilmore, Lumsden Hare and Alfred Hickman
Opened: March 11, 1909 (1 perf.)

An American Widow — a comedy by Kellett Chambers
Produced by: Edgar Selwyn
Cast included: Frederick Perry and Joseph Adelman
Opened: September 6, 1909 (32 perfs.)

On the Eve — a drama of Modern Russian Life by Martha Morton from the German of Leopold Kampf
Produced by: Frank Keenan
Cast included: Joseph Adelman, Minna Adelman and Frank Keenan
Opened: October 4, 1909 (24 perfs.)

The Builder of Bridges — by Alfred Sutro
Produced by: William Seymour
Cast included: DeWitt C. Jennings and Kyrle Bellew
Opened: October 26, 1909 (47 perfs.)

Arsene Lupin — by François de Croisset and Maurice Le Blanc
Produced by: William Seymour
Cast included: Beverly Sitgreaves, Charles Harbury and William Courtenay
Opened: Lyceum/August 26, 1909; Hudson/December 13, 1909 (144 perfs.)

The Next of Kin — by Charles Klein
Produced by: Henry B. Harris
Cast included: Joseph Adelman, Minna Adelman, Hedwig Reicher, Frederick Perry, Harry Davenport, Wallace Eddinger and Maggie Fielding
Opened: December 27, 1909 (24 perfs.)

1910

Henry B. Harris and partner Jesse Lasky opened their new Folies Bergère at 210 West 46th Street on April 27, 1911, as a combination music hall and restaurant. The venture didn't work and on October 20, 1911, they reopened the property as a legitimate playhouse named the Fulton Theatre. It later became the Helen Hayes Theatre.

Plays Presented at the Hudson this Year:

A Lucky Star — a farce by Anne Crawford Flexner from the novel "The Motor Chaperon" by C. N. and A. M. Williamson
Produced by: William Collier
Cast included: William Collier, William "Buster" Collier, Jr. and Marjorie Wood
Opened: January 18, 1910 (95 perfs.)

The Spendthrift — by Porter Emerson Browne
Produced by: Frederic Thompson
Cast included: Edmund Breese and Thais Magrane
Opened: April 11, 1910 (88 perfs.)

The Deserters — by Robert Peyton Carter and Anna Alice Chapin
Produced by: Henry B. Harris
Directed by: Frank Reicher
Cast included: Frederick Truesdell, Helen Ware and James J. Ryan
Opened: September 20, 1910 (63 perfs.)

Nobody's Widow — a farcical romance by Avery Hopwood
Produced by: David Belasco
Cast included: Blanche Bates, Adelaide Prince and Bruce McRae
Opened: November 15, 1910 (215 perfs.)

1911

Plays Presented at the Hudson this Year:

Snobs — by George Bronson-Howard
Produced by: Henry B. Harris
Cast included: Reginald Hughston and Frank J. McIntyre
Opened: September 4, 1911 (64 perfs.)

The Price — by George H. Broadhurst
Produced by: Henry B. Harris
Cast included: Warner Oland, George W. Barnum, Jessie Ralph and Helen Ware

Opened: November 1, 1911 (77 perfs.)

1912

Henry B. Harris died in the early morning of April 15, 1912 along with 1,500 other passengers who were aboard the Titanic.

Plays Presented at the Hudson this Year:

The Return from Jerusalem — by Owen Johnson from the French of Maurice Donnay
Cast included: Madame Simone, Belle Starr and Geoffrey Stein
Opened: January 10, 1912 (53 perfs.)

The Lady of Dreams — by Louis N. Parker from the French of Edmond Rostand
Cast included: Madame Simone, Geoffrey Stein and Margaret Wycherly
Opened: February 28, 1912 (21 perfs.)

Frou-Frou — by Harrison Grey Fiske from the French of Henri Meilhac and Ludovic Halévy
Produced by: Liebler & Co.
Cast included: Madame Simone and Julia Taylor
Opened: March 18, 1912 (8 perfs.)

The Right to be Happy — by H. Kellett Chambers
Produced by: Henry B. Harris
Cast included: Edmund Breese, Dorothy Donnelly, and Louise Galloway
Opened: March 26, 1912 (31 perfs.)

The Typhoon — by Emil Nyitray and Byron Ongley from the Hungarian of Menyhert Lengyel
Produced by: Walker Whiteside
Cast included: Henry Bergman, Florence Reed and Walker Whiteside

Opened: Fulton/March 11, 1912; Hudson/April 22, 1912 (96 perfs.)

Honest Jim Blunt — by William Boden
Produced by: Liebler & Co.
Cast included: Louise Closser Hale, Violet Heming and Charles Laite
Opened: September 16, 1912 (16 perfs.)

Man and Superman — by George Bernard Shaw
Produced by: Liebler & Co.
Cast included: May Seton and Sydney Valentine
Opened: September 30, 1912 (32 perfs.)

The Trial Marriage — by Elmer Harris
Produced by: the estate of Henry B. Harris
Directed by: Edward Elsner
Cast included: Helen Ware, Harry Lillford, Ernest Stallard and Charles A. Stevenson
Opened: October 29, 1912 (23 perfs.)

The High Road — by Edward Sheldon
Produced by: Harrison Grey Fiske and Mrs. Fiske
Directed by: Harrison Grey Fiske and Mrs. Fiske
Cast included: Mrs. Fiske, Arthur Byron and Frederick Perry
Opened: November 19, 1912 (71 perfs.)

1913
Plays Presented at the Hudson this Year:

Nan — by John Masefield
Produced by: Stage Society of New York
Cast included: Albert E. Anson, Constance Collier, Ivan F. Simpson and Henry Stephenson
Opened: January 13, 1913 (1 matinee perf.)

Poor Little Rich Girl — a play of fact and fancy by Eleanor Gates
Produced by: Mr. Richard Walton Tully
Cast included: Alan Hale and Viola Dana

Opened: January 21, 1913 (160 perfs.)

The Fight — by Bayard Veiller
Produced by: Mr. Holbrook Blinn
Cast included: Margaret Wycherly, Malcolm Duncan and Marjorie Wood
Opened: September 2, 1913 (80 perfs.)

General John Regan — by George A. Birmingham
Produced by: Mr. Felix Edwardes
Cast included: Richard Sullivan, John M. O'Brien, Arnold Daly and Albert Andrews
Opened: Hudson/November 10, 1913; Liberty/January 5, 1914 (72 perfs.)

1914
Plays Presented at the Hudson this Year:

A Little Water on the Side — a comedy by William Collier and Grant Stewart
Produced by: Charles Frohman
Cast included: William Collier, William "Buster" Collier, Jr., Charles Dow Clark and Grant Stewart
Opened: January 6, 1914 (63 perfs.)

What Would You Do — by Augustin MacHugh
Produced by: John L. Arthur
Directed by: John L. Arthur
Cast included: Louise Drew, Alice Carrington, Karl Ritter and John L. Arthur
Opened: March 12, 1914 (16 perfs.)

As You Like It — by William Shakespeare
Twelfth Night — by William Shakespeare
The Taming of the Shrew — by William Shakespeare
Produced by: Margaret Anglin
Cast included: Margaret Anglin and Sydney Greenstreet

Opened: March 16, 1914 (perfs. unknown)
NB. In 1913 Margaret Anglin Repertory went on tour with these three productions plus Antony and Cleopatra, returning to New York City and the Hudson in 1914.

Lady Windermere's Fan — by Oscar Wilde
Produced by: George Foster Platt
Cast included: Sydney Greenstreet, Margaret Anglin, Pedro de Cordoba and Wallace Widdecombe
Opened: Hudson/March 30, 1914; Liberty/April 13, 1914 (72 perfs.)

The Dummy — a detective comedy by Harvey J. O'Higgins and Harriet Ford
Produced by: T. Daniel Frawley
Cast included: Frank Connor and Joseph Brennan
Opened: April 13, 1914 (200 perfs.)
NB. A young (age 11) Claire Booth Luce was the understudy for "Little Girl".

The Heart of a Thief — by Paul Armstrong
Produced by: Paul Armstrong
Cast included: Martha Hedman and Anne Sutherland
Opened: October 5, 1914 (8 perfs.)

A Perfect Lady — a comedy by Channing Pollock and Rennold Wolf
Produced by: Robert Milton
Cast included: Rose Stahl, James Cody and Louis Mason
Opened: October 28, 1914 (21 perfs.)

The Big Idea — by A. E. Thomas and Clayton Hamilton
Produced by: Sam Forrest and Charles Gilmore
Cast included: Ernest Glendinning, Forrest Robinson, William Courtleigh and Richard Sterling
Opened: November 16, 1914 (24 perfs.)

The Show Shop — by James Forbes
Produced by: James Forbes

Cast included: Douglas Fairbanks
Opened: December 31, 1914 (156 perfs.)

1915
Plays Presented at the Hudson this Year:

Alice in Wonderland — dramatized by Alice Gerstenberg from the novels by Lewis Carroll
Produced by: W. H. Gilmore
Cast included: Winifred Hanley, Walter Kingsford, Geoffrey Stein, Frank Stirling and Tommy and Vivian Tobin
Opened: Booth/March 23, 1915; Hudson/April 5, 1915 (25 perfs.)

Under Fire — by Roi Cooper Megrue
Produced by: Roi Cooper Megrue and William Courtenay
Directed by: Roi Cooper Megrue and William Courtenay
Cast included: William Courtenay, Edward G. Robinson, Violet Heming and Henry Stephenson
Opened: August 12, 1915 (129 perfs.)

1916
Plays Presented at the Hudson this Year:

Bunny — by Austin Strong
Produced by: Austin Strong
Directed by: Austin Strong
Cast included: Eva Le Gallienne, Lewis S. Stone, Harold Hubert and Henry Stephenson
Opened: January 4, 1916 (16 perfs.)

The Cinderella Man — a comedy by Edward Childs Carpenter and Helen K. Carpenter
Produced by: Victor Herbert and Robert Milton
Cast included: Frank Bacon, Charles Lane, Reginald Mason and Hazel Turney
Opened: January 17, 1916 (192 perfs.)

Pollyanna — a comedy by Catherine Chisholm Cushing based on the novel by Eleanor H. Porter
Produced by: Frederick Stanhope
Cast included: Philip Merivale, Patricia Collinge, Herbert Kelcey and Effie Shannon
Opened: September 18, 1916 (112 perfs.)

Shirley Kaye — a comedy by Hulbert Footner
Produced by: Edgar MacGregor
Cast included: Elsie Ferguson, William Holden, Helen Erskine and Lee Baker
Opened: December 25, 1916 (88 perfs.)

1917
Plays Presented at the Hudson this Year:

Our Betters — a comedy by W. Somerset Maugham
Produced by: J. Clifford Booke
Directed by: J. Clifford Booke
Cast included: Chrystal Herne, Leonore Harris and John Flood
Opened: March 12, 1917 (112 perfs.)

The Deluge — by Frank Allen from the Scandinavian of Henning Berger
Produced by: Arthur Hopkins
Cast included: Edward G. Robinson, Pauline Lord, William Dick and Robert McWade
Opened: August 20, 1917 (16 perfs.)

Good Night, Paul — a musical farce by Roland Oliver and Charles Dickson
Produced by: J. Harry Benrimo
Directed by: J. Harry Benrimo
Cast included: Elizabeth Murray and Ralph C. Herz
Opened: September 3, 1917 (40 perfs.)

The Rescuing Angel — by Clare Kummer
Produced by: Arthur Hopkins

Cast included: Billie Burke, Robert McWade and Frederick Perry
Opened: October 8, 1917 (32 perfs.)

The Pipes of Pan — a comedy by Edward Childs Carpenter
Produced by: Selwyn & Co.
Cast included: Edith King, Norman Trevor and Henry Travers
Opened: November 6, 1917 (87 perfs.)

1918

On May 5, 1918, the Hudson held the 29th Annual Entertainment in aid of the relief fund for the Treasurers Club of America. The Lambs Gambol was held at the Hudson this year. The Lambs raised money for charity and engaged in various civil activities in aid of the war. Mrs.Harris donated the Hudson to the Lambs for their series of performances and paid for the events.

Plays Presented at the Hudson this Year:

The Indestructible Wife — a comedy by Frederic and Fanny Hatton
Produced by: John Cromwell
Cast included: Minna Gombel, Lionel Atwill and John Cromwell
Opened: January 30, 1918 (22 perfs.)

The Master — a comedy adapted by Benjamin F. Glazer from the German of Hermann Bahr
Produced by: Arnold Daly
Cast included: Arnold Daly, Ann Andrews, George Frederic and Harry Mestayer
Opened: February 18, 1918 (39 perfs.)

Democracy's King — by Arnold Daly
Produced by: Arnold Daly
Cast included: Arnold Daly, George Frederic, William Frederic and Harry Mestayer
Opened: February 18, 1918 (15 perfs.)

Nancy Lee — by Eugene Walter and H. Crownin Wilson
Produced by: Mrs. Henry B. Harris

Directed by: Mrs. Henry B. Harris
Cast included: Charlotte Walker and Charles MacDonald
Opened: April 9, 1918 (63 perfs.)

Friendly Enemies — a comedy drama by Samuel Shipman and Aaron Hoffman
Produced by: A. H. Woods and Robert Milton
Cast included: Felix Krembs, Louis Mann and Sam Bernard
Opened: July 22, 1918 (440 perfs.)

1919
Plays Presented at the Hudson this Year:

Clarence — a comedy by Booth Tarkington
Produced by: George C. Tyler
Directed by: Frederick Stanhope
Cast included: John Flood, Mary Boland, Glenn Hunter, Helen Hayes and Alfred Lunt
Opened: September 20, 1919 (300 perfs.)

1920
Plays Presented at the Hudson this Year:

Crooked Gamblers — a comedy drama by Samuel Shipman and Percival Wilde
Produced by: A. H. Woods
Directed by: Robert Milton
Cast included: Edward Fielding, Maude Hanaford, William B. Mack and Robert McWade
Opened: July 31, 1920 (82 perfs.)

The Meanest Man in the World — by Augustin MacHugh based on a skit by Everett Ruskay
Produced by: George M. Cohan
Cast included: George M. Cohan, Ruth Donnelly, Leona Hogarth and Frank M. Thomas
Opened: October 12, 1920 (202 perfs.)

1921

Plays Presented at the Hudson this Year:

Nemesis — by Augustus Thomas
Produced by: George M. Cohan
Directed by: John Meehan
Cast included: Pedro de Cordoba, Emmett Corrigan,
  Robert Cummings, Jerry Hart and Eleanor Woodruff
Opened: April 4, 1921 (56 perfs.)

The Tavern — by Cora Dick Gantt
Produced by: George M. Cohan
Directed by: George M. Cohan and John Meehan
Cast included: Eugenie Blair, George M. Cohan and Isabel Withers
Opened: George M. Cohan Theatre/September 27, 1920
t hen Hudson/May 23, 1921 (279 perfs.)

The Poppy God — by Leon Gordon, Leroy Clements
  and Thomas Grant Springer
Produced by: The Selwyns
Cast included: Wallace Ford, Ruby Gordon and Ralph Morgan
Opened: August 29, 1921 (16 perfs.)

The Man in the Making — by James W. Elliott
Produced by: John Meehan, Inc.
Directed by: John Meehan
Cast included: Francis Byrne, Kathleen Comegys, William B. Mack
  and Susanne Willis
Opened: September 20, 1921 (22 perfs.)

The Six-Fifty — by Kate McLaurin
Produced by: Lee Kugel
Cast included: Lillian Albertson, Lillian Ross and Hazel Turny
Opened: October 24, 1921 (24 perfs.)

The Varying Shore — by Zoe Akins
Produced by: Sam H. Harris
Directed by: Sam Forrest

Cast included: Charles Baldwin, Donald Bethune, Elsie Ferguson, Geraldine O'Brien and Rollo Peters
Opened: December 5, 1921 (66 perfs.)

1922
Plays Presented at the Hudson this Year:

The Voice from the Minaret — by Robert Hichens
Produced by: Marie Löhr
Directed by: Marie Löhr
Cast included: Herbert Marshall, Edmund Gwen, Content Paleolobue and Marie Löhr
Opened: January 30, 1922 (13 perfs.)
NB. The play came to the Hudson from the Globe Theatre in London.

Fedora — a drama — by Victorien Sardou
Produced by: Marie Löhr
Directed by: Marie Löhr
Cast included: Herbert Marshall, Edmund Gwen and Marie Löhr
Opened: February 10, 1922 (12 perfs.)

The Rubicon — a comedy by Henry Baron from the French of Edouard Bourdet
Produced by: Clifford Brooke
Directed by: Clifford Brooke
Cast included: Violet Heming, Warburton Gamble and Kenneth Hill
Opened: February 21, 1922 (135 perfs.)

So This is London — a comedy by Arthur F. Goodrich
Produced by: John Meehan and George M. Cohan
Directed by: John Meehan
Cast included: Edmund Breese, Lily Cahill, Donald Gallaher and Lawrence D'Orsay
Opened: August 30, 1922 (357 perfs.)

1923
Plays Presented at the Hudson this Year:

The Crooked Square — by Samuel Shipman and Alfred C. Kennedy
Produced by: Fred G. Stanhope
Directed by: Fred G. Stanhope
Cast included: Jack LaRue and Edna Hibbard
Opened: September 10, 1923 (88 perfs.)

Sancho Panza — by Menyhert Lengyel from episodes in
 "Don Quixote" by Miguel de Cervantes
Produced by: Richard Boleslawsky and Russell Janney
Cast included: Otis Skinner and Robert Robson
Opened: November 26, 1923 (40 perfs.)

The Song and Dance Man — a dramatic comedy by George M. Cohan
Produced by: George M. Cohan
Cast included: Louis Calhern, Robert Cummings, George M. Cohan,
 Lynne Overman, Frederick Perry and John Meehan
Opened: December 31, 1923 (96 perfs.)

1924
Plays Presented at the Hudson this Year:

Across the Street — by Richard A. Purdy
Produced by: Oliver Morosco
Directed by: Oliver Morosco
Cast included: Robert Emmett Keane, Fred Raymond
 and Ruth Thomas
Opened: March 24, 1924 (32 perfs.)

Cobra — by Martin Brown
Produced by: L. Lawrence Weber
Cast included: Louise Calhern, William B. Mack, Ralph Morgan
 and Judith Anderson
Opened: April 22, 1924 (240 perfs.)

High Stakes — by Willard Mack
Produced by: A. H. Woods
Cast included: Wilton Lackaye and Phoebe Foster
Opened: September 9, 1924 (120 perfs.)

The Fake — by Frederick Lonsdale
Produced by: A. H. Woods
Cast included: Frieda Inescort, John Williams and Una O'Connor
Opened: October 6, 1924 (89 perfs.)

The Bully — by Julie Helene Percival and Calvin Clark
Produced by: Mrs. Henry B. Harris
Cast included: Emmett Corrigan and Olive Oliver
Opened: December 25, 1924 (36 perfs.)

1925
Plays Presented at the Hudson this Year:

Out of Step — by A. A. Kline
Produced by: The Dramatists Theatre, Inc.
Cast included: Muriel Kirkland, Eric Dressler and Marcia Byron
Opened: January 29, 1925 (21 perfs.)

Houses of Sand — by G. Marion Burton
Produced by: Michael Mindlin
Cast included: Charles A. Bickford, Paul Kelly and Edith Shayne
Opened: February 17, 1925 (31 perfs.)

The Devil Within — by Charles Horan
Produced by: Rock & Horan, Inc.
Cast included: William Ingersoll and Henry W. Pemberton
Opened: March 16, 1925 (24 perfs.)

The Backslapper — by Paul Dickey and Mann Page
Produced by: John Henry Mears and Paul Dickey
Cast included: Roger Pryor, Jack Daniels and Mary Fowler
Opened: April 11, 1925 (33 perfs.)

His Queen — by John Hastings Turner
Produced by: Oliver Morosco
Directed by: Oliver Morosco
Cast included: Francine Larrimore and Charles Brown
Opened: May 11, 1925 (11 perfs.)

The Morning After — by Len D. Hollister and Leona Stephens
Produced by: L. M. Simmons
Directed by: Lester Lonigan
Cast included: Verree Teasdale, Arthur Aylsworth
 and A. H. Van Buren
Opened: July 27, 1925 (24 perfs.)

American Born — by George M. Cohan
Produced by: George M. Cohan
Directed by: George M. Cohan
Cast included: George M. Cohan and Lorna Lawrence
Opened: October 5, 1925 (88 perfs.)

1926
Plays Presented at the Hudson this Year:

The Home Towners — by George M. Cohan
Produced by: George M. Cohan
Directed by: John Meehan
Cast included: Robert McWade, Chester Morris and William Elliott
Opened: August 23, 1926 (64 perfs.)

The Noose — by Willard Mack from a story by Herbert H. Van Loan
Produced by: Mrs. Henry B. Harris
Directed by: Willard Mack
Cast included: Barbara Stanwyck and Ann Shoemaker
Opened: October 20, 1926 (197 perfs.)

1927
Plays Presented at the Hudson this Year:

Wall Street — by James N. Rosenberg
Produced by: The Stagers
Cast included: John Warner, John McGovern, Samuel Levene and Henry Brown
Opened: April 20, 1927 (21 perfs.)

Kempy — by J. C. Nugent and Elliott Nugent
Produced by: Murray Phillips
Directed by: J. C. Nugent
Cast included: Ruth Nugent, J. C. Nugent and Elliott Nugent
Opened: May 11, 1927 (48 perfs.)

Blood Money — by George Middleton from a story by Herbert H. Van Loan
Produced by: Mrs. Henry B. Harris
Cast included: Kate McComb, Phyllis Povah and Thomas Mitchell
Opened: August 22, 1927 (64 perfs.)

Weather Clear - Track Fast — by Willard Mack
Produced by: Willard Mack
Directed by: Willard Mack
Cast included: Jim Bubbles, Joe Laurie, Jr. and William Courtleigh
Opened: October 18, 1927 (63 perfs.)

The Plough and the Stars — by Sean O'Casey
Produced by: George C. Tyler
Directed by: Arthur Sinclair
Cast included: Sara Allgood, Tony Quinn and Arthur Sinclair
Opened: November 28, 1927 (48 perfs.)

Los Angeles — by Max Marcin and Donald Ogden Stewart
Produced by: George M. Cohan
Cast included: Frances Dale, Alison Skipworth, Jack LaRue and Helen Vinson
Opened: December 19, 1927 (16 perfs.)

1928

Mrs. Harris temporarily retired from managing the Hudson and producing plays to take a world tour. She leased the theater to Howard Schnebbe.

Plays Presented at the Hudson this Year:

A Distant Drum — by Vincent Lawrence
Produced by: William H. Harris, Jr.
Directed by: William H. Harris, Jr.
Cast included: Felix Krembs, Mary Newcomb and Louis Calhern
Opened: January 20, 1928 (11 perfs.)

Whispering Friends — by George M. Cohan
Produced by: George M. Cohan
Cast included: Chester Morris, Elsie Lawson, William Harrigan
  and Anne Shoemaker
Opened: February 20, 1928 (112 perfs.)

Goin' Home — by Ransom Rideout
Produced by: Brock Pemberton
Directed by: Brock Pemberton and Antoinette Perry
Cast included: Georges Renavent, Richard Hale
  and Barbara Bulgakova
Opened: August 23, 1928 (77 perfs.)

By Request — by J. C. Nugent and Elliott Nugent
Produced by: George M. Cohan
Directed by: J. C. Nugent and Elliott Nugent
Cast included: Elliott Nugent, J. C. Nugent and Verree Teasdale
Opened: September 27, 1928 (28 perfs.)

To-night at 12 —by Owen Davis
Produced by: Herman Shumlin
Directed by: Melville Burke
Cast included: Spring Byington and Owen Davis, Jr.
Opened: November 13, 1928 (60 perfs.)

1929
Plays Presented at the Hudson this Year:

Appearances — by Garland Anderson
Produced by: C. Mischell Picard
Directed by: Lee Miller
Cast included: Harry Bond, Hazel Gray and Jerome Wise
Opened: April 1, 1929 (24 perfs.)

Messin' Around — music by Jimmy Johnson and lyrics by Perry Bradford
Produced by: Louis I. Isquith
Directed by: Louis I. Isquith and Eddie Rector
Ensemble included: Walter Brogsdale, Emma Maitland and Lena Shadney
Opened: April 22, 1929 (33 perfs.)

Hot Chocolates — music by Thomas "Fats" Waller and Harry Brooks with lyrics by Andy Razaf
Directed by: Leonard Harper
Ensemble included: Louis Armstrong, Baby Cox, Edith Wilson, Russell Wooding's Jubilee Singers, Three Midnight Steppers, and Jazzlips Richardson and the Six Crackerjacks
Opened: June 20, 1929 (219 perfs.)
Gangster Dutch Schulz helped finance Hot Chocolate's move to Broadway.

City Haul — by Elizabeth Miele
Produced by: Gil Boag
Cast included: Mathilda Baring, Lizzie McCall, Gene Miller and Ann Winston
Opened: December 30, 1929 (77 perfs.)

1930
Plays Presented at the Hudson this Year:

Troyka —by Lula Vollmer from the Hungarian of Imre Fazekas

Produced by: Laura D. Wilck
Directed by: Lemist Esler
Cast included: Zita Johann, Jack Roseleigh and Albert Van Dekker
Opened: April 1, 1930 (15 perfs.)

Virtue's Bed — by Courtenay Savage
Produced by: Lohmuller and Emery, Inc.
Cast included: Ara Gerald and Robert Strange
Opened: April 15, 1930 (71 perfs.)

Bad Girl — by Brian Marlow and Vina Delmar
Produced by: Robert V. Newman
Cast included: Paul Kelly and Sylvia Sidney
Opened: October 2, 1930 (85 perfs.)

The Inspector General — a satirical farce by John Anderson from the Russian of Nikolai Gogol
Produced by: Jed Harris
Directed by: Jed Harris
Cast included: Dorothy Gish, J. Edward Bromberg and Romney Brent
Opened: December 23, 1930 (7 perfs.)

1931
Plays Presented at the Hudson this Year:

Doctor X — by Howard Warren Comstock and Allen C. Miller
Produced by: William Brandt and Harry Brandt
Directed by: Josephine Victor
Cast included: Howard Lang
Opened: February 9, 1931 (80 perfs.)

Perfectly Scandalous — by Hutcheson Boyd
Produced by: Ray Gallo
Cast included: Henry W. Pemberton, Natalie Shafer and Jeanne Greene
Opened: May 13, 1931 (5 perfs.)

A Regular Guy — by Patrick Kearney
Produced by: Jules J. Leventhal
Directed by: Patrick Kearney
Cast included: Charlotte Wynters and Edward Pawley
Opened: June 4, 1931 (13 perfs.)

Old Man Murphy — by Patrick Kearney and Harry Wagstaff Gribble
Produced by: Robert V. Newman
Directed by: Harry Wagstaff Gribble and Lawrence Bolton
Cast included: Peggy Conklin, Arthur Sinclair and Henry O'Neill
Opened: September 14, 1931 (48 perfs.)

Enemy Within — by Will Piper and Lois Howell
Produced by: Roy Walling
Directed by: Roy Walling
Cast included: Walter N. Greaza and Anne Forrest
Opened: October 5, 1931 (8 perfs.)

Miss Gulliver Travels — by George Ford and Ethel Taylor
Produced by: George Ford
Directed by: Ethel Taylor
Cast included: James Benton, Leslie Hunt and P. J. Kelly
Opened: November 25, 1931 (21 perfs.)

1932
Plays Presented at the Hudson this Year:

Never No More — by James Knox Millen
Directed by: Chester Erskin
Cast included: Viola Dean, Rose McClendon and Lew Payton
Opened: January 7, 1932 (12 perfs.)

The Budget — by Robert Middlemass
Produced by: Harry Askin and Hugh Ford
Directed by: Hugh Ford
Cast included: Virginia Curley, John M. Kline, Mary Lawlor,
  Lynne Overman and Raymond Walburn

Opened: September 20, 1932 (7 perfs.)

The Show Off — by George Kelly
Produced by: Jules J. Leventhal and O. E. Wee
Directed by: Raymond Walburn
Cast included: Jean Adair, Charles Martin, Frances McHugh and Raymond Walburn
Opened: December 12, 1932 (119 perfs.)

1933
Plays Presented at the Hudson this Year:

Riddle Me This — by Daniel N. Rubin
Produced by: Jules J. Leventhal and O. E. Wee
Cast included: Frank Allworth, Earl Redding and Virginia Stevens
Opened: March 14, 1933 (70 perfs.)

It's a Wise Child — by Laurence E. Johnson
Produced by: Jules J. Leventhal and O. E. Wee
Cast included: Harlan Briggs, Geraldine Brown and Hugh Cameron
Opened: May 16, 1933 (34 perfs.)

Eight Bells — by Percy G. Mandley
Produced by: A. C. Blumenthal
Directed by: Frank Gregory
Cast included: Harrison Brockbank, David Hughes and Eric West
Opened: October 28, 1933 (17 perfs.)

1934-1936
(No plays opened at the Hudson during these years.)

Columbia Broadcasting System purchased the property and aired its first CBS Radio Playhouse on February 3, 1934, making radio history with the first radio broadcast with a live studio audience.

1937
CBS returns the facility to its former name—the Hudson—and new

managers Sam H. Grisman and Jack Kirkland reintroduce the Hudson as a legitimate playhouse.

Plays Presented at the Hudson this Year:

An Enemy of the People — by Henrik Ibsen
Produced by: Walter Hampden
Directed by: Walter Hampden
Cast included: Charles Brunswick, Walter Hampden and Mabel Moore
Opened: February 15, 1937 (16 perfs.)

The Amazing Dr. Clitterhouse — by Barre Lyndon
Produced by: Gilbert Miller with Warner Brothers
Cast included: Clarence Derwent, Cedric Hardwicke, Muriel Hutchison and Ernest Jay
Opened: March 2, 1937 (80 perfs.)

Too Many Heroes — by Dore Schary
Produced by: Carly Wharton
Directed by: Garson Kanin
Cast included: James Backus, Shirley Booth, Clyde Franklin and Marion Willis
Opened: November 15, 1937 (16 perfs.)

Western Waters — by Richard Carlson with incidental music by Lehman Engel
Produced by: Elsa Moses
Directed by: Elsa Moses and Richard Carlson
Cast included: Van Heflin, Mabel Paige and Maxine Stuart
Opened: December 28, 1937 (7 perfs.)

1938

Plays Presented at the Hudson this Year:

Sunup to Sundown — by Francis Edwards Faragoh
Produced by: D. A. Doran

Cast included: Leslie Barrett, Walter N. Greaza, Sydney Lumet
and Margaret Moore
Opened: February 1, 1938 (7 perfs.)

Who's Who — by Leonard Sillman and Everett Marcy
Music by: Baldwin Bergersen, James Shelton, Irvin Graham
and Paul McGrane
Lyrics by: June Sillman, Irvin Graham and James Shelton
Produced by: Elsa Maxwell
Cast included: Imogene Coca, Rags Ragland, James Shelton,
June Sillman and Elizabeth Wilde
Opened: March 1, 1938 (23 perfs.)

Whiteoaks — by Mazo de la Roche from her book series "Whiteoaks of Jalna"
Produced by: Victor Payne-Jennings
Cast included: Ethel Barrymore, Ethel Colt and Olive Reeves-Smith
Opened: March 23, 1938 (112 perfs.)

Thirty Days Hath September — by Irving Gaumont and Jack Sobell
Produced by: Kirby Grant, Inc.
Cast included: Nat Burns, Alice Fleming, Julia Johnston
and Elisabeth Wilde
Opened: September 30, 1938 (16 perfs.)

Waltz in Goose Step — by Oliver H. P. Garrett
Produced by: Julien Chaqueneau
Directed by: Arthur Hopkins
Cast included: France Bendtsen, Mariana Fiory, Barrie Wanless
and Palmer Ward
Opened: November 1, 1938 (7 perfs.)

Good Hunting — by Nathanael West and Joseph Schrank
Produced by: Jerome Mayer and Leonard Field
Cast included: Marcel Journet, Susi Lanner and Estelle Winwood
Opened: November 21, 1938 (2 perfs.)

1939
Plays Presented at the Hudson this Year:

The Coggerers — believed to be by Paul Vincent Carroll
Produced by: One-Act Repertory Company with Sam H. Grisman
Cast included: Horton Foote, Lionel Ince and Irene Oshier
Opened: January 20, 1939 (3 perfs.)

Mr. Banks of Birmingham — (author unknown)
Produced by: One-Act Repertory Company with Sam H. Grisman
Cast included: Horton Foote, Walter N. Greaza, Lionel Ince
 and Vera Visconti
Opened: January 20, 1939 (3 perfs.)

The Red Velvet Goat — believed to be by Josephina Niggli
Produced by: One-Act Repertory Company with Sam H. Grisman
Cast included: Horton Foote, Walter N. Greaza, Lionel Ince
 and Vera Visconti
Opened: January 20, 1939 (3 perfs.)

Lew Leslie's Blackbirds of 1939 — by Lew Leslie with lyrics
 by Johnny Mercer
Produced by: Lew Leslie
Cast included: Lena Horne, Rosalie King and Lavinia Williams
Opened: February 11, 1939 (9 perfs.)

I Know What I Like — by Justin Sturm
Produced by: T. Edward Hambleton and Richard Skinner
Scenic design by: Donald Oenslager
Cast included: Edward Broadley, Frank Brown and Haila Stoddard
Opened: November 24, 1939 (11 perfs.)

1940
Plays Presented at the Hudson this Year:

Grey Farm — by Hector Bolitho and Terence Rattigan
Produced by: Irving Cooper

Directed by: Berthold
Cast included: John Cromwell, Oscar Homolka
 and Vera Fuller Mellish
Opened: May 3, 1940 (35 perfs.)

Love for Love — by William Congreve with a prologue and epilogue by Charles Hanson Towne
Produced by: The Players
Directed by: Robert Edmond Jones
Incidental music by: Macklin Marrow
Scenic design by: Robert Edmond Jones
Cast included: Romney Brent, Leo G. Carroll, Bobby Clark,
 Dudley Digges, Dorothy Gish, Walter Hampden, Violet Heming,
 Cornelia Otis Skinner and Peggy Wood
Opened: June 3, 1940 (8 perfs.)

Fledgling — by Charles Chilton and Philip Lewis based on the play "Follow the Fun" by Charles Chilton
Produced by: Otis Chatfield-Taylor
Directed by: Heinrich Schnitzler
Cast included: Norma Chambers, Margaret Clifford, Ralph Morgan
 and Sylvia Weld
Opened: November 27, 1940 (13 perfs.)

1941
Plays Presented at the Hudson this Year:

Night of Love — by Rowland Leigh adapted from the Hungarian
 by Lili Hatvany
Produced by: Lee Shubert and J. J. Shubert
Directed by: Barry O'Daniels
Music: Robert Stolz (music), Rowland Leigh (lyrics), George Lessner
 (orchestration), Joseph Littau (Musical Director)
Cast included: Robert Chisholm, Sally Evans and Helen Gleason
Opened: January 7, 1941 (7 perfs.)

My Fair Ladies — by Arthur L. Jarrett and Marcel Klauber

Produced by: Albert Lewis and Max Siegel
Cast included: Betty Furness, Celeste Holm, Lionel Ince, Jacqueline Susann, Henry Vincent and Herbert Yost
Opened: March 23, 1941 (32 perfs.)

All Men Are Alike — by Vernon Sylvaine
Produced by: Lee Ephraim
Cast included: Bobby Clark, Reginald Denny, Ethel Morrison and Mary Newnham-Davis
Opened: October 6, 1941 (32 perfs.)

Theatre — by Guy Bolton and W. Somerset Maugham
Produced by: John Golden
Directed by: John Golden
Scenic design by: Donald Oenslager
Cast included: Cornelia Otis Skinner, Helen Flint and John Moore
Opened: November 12, 1941 (69 perfs.)

1942

Robert and Wilva Breen begin their long run as tenants in the apartment over the marquee of the Hudson Theatre.

Plays Presented at the Hudson this Year:

Jason — by Samson Raphaelson
Produced by: George Abbott
Directed by: Samson Raphaelson
Cast included: Nicholas Conte, E. G. Marshall, Tom Tully, Helen Walker and Edna West
Opened: January 21, 1942 (125 perfs.)

Uncle Harry — by Thomas Job
Produced by: Clifford Hayman with Lennie Hatten
Directed by: Lem Ward
Cast included: Eva Le Gallienne, Joseph Schildkraut, A. P. Kaye and Karl Malden
Opened: May 20, 1942 (430 perfs.)

1943
Plays Presented at the Hudson this Year:

Run, Little Chillun — by Hall Johnson
Produced by: Lew Cooper, Meyer Davis and George Jessel
Cast included: Miriam Burton, Freyde Marshall, Wardell Saunders and Eloise Uggams
Opened: August 11, 1943 (16 perfs.)

Arsenic and Old Lace — by Joseph Kesselring
Produced by: Howard Lindsay and Russel Crouse
Cast included: Jean Adair, John Alexander, Josephine Hull, Boris Karloff and Victor Sutherland
Opened: Fulton/January 10, 1941 then Hudson/September 25, 1943 (1,444 perfs.)

1944
Plays Presented at the Hudson this Year:

Love on Leave — by A. B. Sheffrin
Produced by: Charles Stewart and Martin Goodman
Cast included: Stanley Bell, Millard Mitchell and Mary Sargent
Opened: June 20, 1944 (7 perfs.)

Snafu — a comedy by Louis Soloman and Harold Buchman
Produced by: George Abbott
Directed by: George Abbott
Cast included: Dort Clark, Eugenia Delarova, Clifford Dunstan, Enid Marke, Ernest Rowan and Winfield Smith
Opened: Hudson/October 25, 1944 then Biltmore/January 1, 1945 (158 perfs.)

1945
Plays Presented at the Hudson this Year:

The Hasty Heart — by John Patrick
Produced by: Howard Lindsay and Russel Crouse

Cast included: Richard Basehart, John Lund and Francis Nielsen
Opened: January 3, 1945 (204 perfs.)

State of the Union — by Howard Lindsay and Russel Crouse
Produced by: Leland Hayward
Cast included: Ralph Bellamy, Kay Johnson, Ruth Hussey, Margalo Gillmore, Myron McCormick and Minor Watson
Opened: November 14, 1945 (765 perfs., closing September 13, 1947)

1946

No new plays opened this year as State of the Union continued its run well into 1947.

1947

Plays Presented at the Hudson this Year:

How I Wonder — by Donald Ogden Stewart
Produced by: Ruth Gordon, Garson Kanin, Victor Samrock and William Fields
Directed by: Garson Kanin
Scenic design by: Donald Oenslager
Costume design by: Helen Pons
Lighting design by: Donald Oenslager
Asst. Stage Manager: Jones Harris
Cast included: Raymond Massey, Carol Goodner, Everett Sloane, Wyrley Birch, Henry Jones, Bethel Leslie, John Marriott, Byron McGrath, Meg Mundy and John Sweet
Opened: September 30, 1947 (63 perfs.)

The Voice of the Turtle — a comedy by John Van Druten
Produced by: Alfred De Liagre, Jr.
Directed by: John Van Druten
Music: Alexander Haas (arranged and conducted)
Press representative: Jean Dalrymple
Cast included: Audrey Christie, Elliott Nugent and Margaret Sullavan
Opened: Morosco/December 8, 1943; Martin Beck/October 15, 1947; and Hudson/November 25, 1947 (1,557 perfs.)

1948
Plays Presented at the Hudson this Year:

Harvest of Years — by DeWitt Bodeen
Produced by: Arthur J. Beckhard
Directed by: Arthur J. Beckhard
Scenic design by: Raymond Sovey
Costume design by: Peggy Morrison
Cast included: Philippa Bevans, Esther Dale, Russell Hardie, Leona Maricle and Lenka Peterson
Opened: January 12, 1948 (16 perfs.)

Man and Superman — by George Bernard Shaw
Produced by: Maurice Evans
Directed by: Maurice Evans and George Schaefer
Scenic design by: Frederick Stover
Costume design by: David Ffolkes
Lighting design by: George Schaefer
Cast included: Maurice Evans, Carmen Mathews and Miriam Stovall
Opened: Alvin/October 8, 1947 then Hudson/February 16, 1948 (295 perfs.)

Set My People Free — by Dorothy Heyward
Produced by: The Theatre Guild
Directed by: Martin Ritt
Cast included: Edith Atuka-Reid, Harry Bolden, Canada Lee, Freyda Marshall and William McDaniel
Opened: November 3, 1948 (29 perfs.)

Jenny Kissed Me — by Jean Kerr
Produced by: James Russo, Michael Ellis and Alexander H. Cohen with Clarence M. Shapiro
Directed by: James Russo
Cast included: Frances Bavier, Ann Baxter, Leo G. Carroll and Camilla De Witt
Opened: December 23, 1948 (20 perfs.)

1949
Plays Presented at the Hudson this Year:

Detective Story — by Sidney S. Kingsley
Produced by: Howard Lindsay and Russel Crouse
Directed by: Sidney S. Kingsley
Cast included: Ralph Bellamy, Meg Mundy, Jean Adair,
  Joan Copeland, Lee Grant, Horace McMahon, Alexander Scourby,
  Maureen Stapleton and Joseph Wiseman
Opened: Hudson/March 23, 1949 then Broadhurst/July 3, 1950
  (581 perfs.)

1950's
No plays opened at the Hudson during these—its television—years.

1960's
Plays Presented at the Hudson this Year:

A Lovely Light — by Dorothy Stickney based on the poetry
  and letters of Edna St. Vincent Millay
Produced by: Solomon Hurok by arrangement with Norma Millay
Directed by: Howard Lindsay
Cast included: Dorothy Stickney (solo performer)
Opened: February 8, 1960 (17 perfs.)

Toys in the Attic — by Lillian Hellman
Produced by: Kermit Bloomgarden
Directed by: Arthur Penn
Cast included: Jason Robards, Jr., Maureen Stapleton, Irene Worth
  and Anne Revere
Opened: February 25, 1960 (456 perfs.)

Becket — translated by Lucienne Hill from the French of Jean Anouilh
Produced by: David Merrick
Directed by: Peter Glenville
Incidental music by: Laurence Rosenthal
Cast included: Arthur Kennedy, Laurence Olivier, James Frawley

and Margaret Hall
Opened: May 8, 1961 (27 perfs.)

Look, We've Come Through — by Hugh Wheeler
Produced by: Frank Prince with David Black and Arnold Saint-Subber
Directed by: José Quintero
Scenic design by: David Hays
Costume design by: Ann Roth
Lighting design by: David Hays
Cast included: Zohra Lampert and Burt Reynolds
Opened: October 25, 1961 (5 perfs.)

Ross — by Terence Rattigan
Produced by: David Merrick
Directed by: Glen Byam Shaw
Cast included: John Mills, Paul Sparer and James Valentine
Opened: Eugene O'Neill/December 26, 1961 then Hudson/April 3, 1962 (159 perfs.)

Strange Interlude — by Eugene O'Neill
Produced by: The Actors Studio with Circle in the Square
Directed by: José Quintero
Cast included: Betty Field, Jane Fonda, Ben Gazzara, Pat Hingle, Geoffrey Horne, Nancy Marchand, Geraldine Page, William Prince, Franchot Tone and Richard Thomas
Opened: Hudson/March 11, 1963 and Martin Beck/May 27, 1963 (98 perfs.)

This Was Burlesque — by Ann Corio with music and lyrics by Sonny Lester and Bill Grundy
Produced by: Michael P. Iannucci
Directed by: Ann Corio
Choreographed by: Paul Morokoff
Cast included: Ann Corio and Dexter Maitland
Opened: March 16, 1965 (124 perfs.)

How to Be a Jewish Mother — by Seymour Vall based on a book by Dan Greenburg
Produced by: Jon-Lee and Seymour Vall
Directed by: Avery Schreiber
Music: Michael Leonard (music), Herbert Martin (lyrics),
  and Julian Stein (arrangement and Musical Director)
Choreographed by: Doug Rogers
Cast included: Godfrey Cambridge, Molly Picon and Naomi Riseman
Opened: December 28, 1967 (32 perfs.)

The Guide — by Harvey Breit and Patricia Rinehart based on
  the novel by R. K. Narayan
Produced by: Noel Weiss
Directed by: George L. Sherman
Cast included: Madhur Jaffrey and Michael Kermoyan
Opened: March 6, 1968 (9 perfs.)

Mike Downstairs — by George Panetta
Produced by: Zev Bufman, Abe Margolies and Edward A. Franck
Directed by: Donald Driver
Incidental music by: Peter Matz
Cast included: Russell Baker, Dane Clark and Edmond Varrato
Opened: April 18, 1968 (15 perfs.)

Author's Note:
Many thanks are owed to numerous sources used to verify and round out the above list including, but in no way limited to, the Internet Broadway Database, the Internet Movie Database, the New York Public Library's website and its CATNYP online catalogue, Ancestry.com, Wikepdia.com, the online Encyclopaedia Britannica, About.com and university library websites such as University of North Carolina.

APPENDIX D

Some of the Guests on *Steve Allen's Tonight Show*

SYLVIA SYMS — Singer
OSCAR PETERSON TRIO — Jazz Unit
STAN FREEMAN — Novelty Pianist
RICHARD HAYMAN — Harmonica Soloist
ELLA FITZGERALD AND TRIO — Jazz Unit
THE CADILLACS — Rock and Roll Vocal Quintet
GENE BAYLOS — Comedian
TOSHIKO — Japanese Jazz Pianist
GREGORY RATOFF — Actor
ROGER RAY — Comedian, Marimba Player
ERNEST BORGNINE — Actor
MIA SLAVENSKA — Prima Ballerina
JUTTA HIPP — German Jazz Pianist
DOUGLAS "WRONG-WAY" CORRIGAN — Old Time Pilot
WILLIE "THE LION" SMITH — Jazz Pianist
TURK MURPHY — Dixieland Trombonist
LUCILLE AND EDDIE ROBERTS — Mind Readers
JULIE LONDON — Singer
DIZZY GILLESPIE AND BAND — Jazz Unit
HENNY YOUNGMAN — Comedian
ELWOOD CARSON — Trick Cyclist
BOB MCFADDEN — Comedian
SONJA HENIE — Actress
COLUMBUS BOYCHOIR — Singing Group
PHIL LEEDS — Comedian
ALLEN FUNT — "Candid-Camera" Films and Interview
THE MODERN JAZZ QUARTET — Jazz Unit
OGDEN NASH — Poet
FRED KEATING — Magician
TITO PUENTE AND BAND — Latin-American Orchestra
LEONA ANDERSON — Novelty Singer
LEW AYRES — Actor
THE AMAZING RANDI — Escape Artist
MEL TORME — Singer
BLACKBURN TWINS — Song and Dance Team

WM. BURKE MILLER, NBC Night Executive Officer — Interview
TEDDY WILSON TRIO — Jazz Unit
KAJAR — Magician
ERSKINE HAWKINS' BAND — Jazz Unit
EDDIE GARSON — Ventriloquist
MARIAN MCPARTLAND TRIO — Jazz Unit
MAE BARNES — Singer
JULIAN "CANNONBALL" ADDERLEY QUINTET — Jazz Unit
JOEY CARTER — Comedian
CHRIS CONNOR — Singer
ART LUND — Singer
GEORGE SHEARING QUINTET — Jazz Unit
ROY ELDRIDGE — Jazz Trumpeter
JULIE WILSON — Singer
CLIFF NORTON — Comedian
RICHARD DYER-BENNETT — Folk Singer
GENE KRUPA QUARTET — Jazz Unit
POLGAR — Hypnotist
DAVE BRUBECK QUARTET — Jazz Unit
ART BLAKEY & HIS JAZZ MESSENGERS — Jazz Unit
DEL RAY — Magician
ARTIE DANN — Comedian
RENZO CEZANO — 'The Continental,' Actor
ARCHER & GILE — Folk Singers
CHAN CANASTA — Mentalist
SISTER ROSETTA THARPE — Gospel Singer
JACK HASKELL — Singer
BARBARA LEA — Singer
CLIFFORD GUEST — Ventriloquist
FLORIAN ZABACH — Violinist
STAN GETZ QUINTET — Jazz Unit
BEATRICE KRAFT — Dancer
ETNAR HANSON — Novelty Musician
THE DENVERS — Knife Throwing Act
BASQUE DANCERS — Spanish Folk Dancers
JIMMY EDMUNDSON — ("Prof. Backwards") Specialty Act
ENID MOSIER & HER TRINIDAD STEEL BAND — Calypso Unit
ENID MARKEY — Actress (Jane in first Tarzan movie)
ROBERT MAXWELL — Harpist
HAZEL SCOTT — Pianist
INK SPOTS — Vocal Quartet
THE CLOVERS — Vocal Quintet

APPENDIX E
"One Thousand and One Events

Interesting events happened at Hotel Macklowe, Macklowe Conference Center and the Hudson Theatre: dramatic product launches attended by hundreds; small meetings with a handful of people locked in tough negotiations; meetings for large companies; meetings for small businesses. In addition to the occasional stage play, the Hudson Theatre hosted corporate and private events that, while not theater in the strict sense, were nonetheless theatrical, spectacular shows in their own unique ways: celebrations, weddings, birthdays, fashion shows, announcement and awards ceremonies. From a book prepared by the Hotel Macklowe called "One Thousand and One Events," here is a glimpse at just some of the successes enjoyed along the way, successes which have continued and grown even brighter as "Discovering the Hudson" relates.

May 24, 1990
Business Executives for National Security

October 8–November 10, 1990
Kasparov vs. Karpov
1990 World Chess Championship

November 12, 1990
BMW Corporate Meeting

December 10, 1990
The Actor's Fund of America presents "A Christmas Carol"

January 29, 1991
Italian Trade Commission, Fashion Show

March 16, 1991
Kips Bay Boys and Girls Club—Cartier Black and White Ball

April 25, 1991
Sony Innovators Awards

June 12, 1991
Microsoft Corporation "Windows on Wall Street"

July 11, 1991
Philip Morris Marlboro Grand Prix Dinner

August 20, 1991
Sylvester Stallone donates to Planet Hollywood

September 23, 1991
UniSys Corporation, Press Conference

September 28, 1991
The New York Times Fashion Exhibits

November 12, 1991
Legprom Export, Russian Textile Exhibit

December 16, 1991
The Actors Fund of America presents "A Christmas Carol"

April 14, 1992
Mazda, Car in a Suitcase

June 24, 1992
New York Knicks NBA Draft Dinner

August 25, 1992
Jimmy Connors 40th Birthday

September 12, 1992
The New York Times Magazine and Cosmair, Inc.,

launches "Gio" de Giorgio Armani

October 16, 1992
Diet Coke 10th Anniversary

November 23, 1992
AMA, The Findings of the Kennedy autopsy

January 29, 1993
Schieffelin and Somerset. Möet and Chandon 250th Anniversary

March 8, 1993
Williamstown Theatre Festival

March 23-24, 1993
Lotus Announces "Lotus Notes Release 3"

April 3, 1993
Gayle Weiner and Cliff Gelbard Wedding

June 6, 1993
"Microsoft At Work"

September 17-21, 1993
Meat Loaf Promotes "Bat Out of Hell: Back Into Hell"

October 2, 1993
Tele-Communications Inc. and Bell Atlantic Merger

October 30, 1993
Starlight Foundation Halloween Ball

January 12, 1994
The Arrow Shirt Company presents The Pointer Sisters

January 13, 1994
Brooklyn Academy of Music Reception for Annie Leibowitz

Index

A. Woollcott 78
Abominable Showman, The 37
Ackerman, John 134
Actors Studio, The 124, 125
Actors' Equity Association 56, 61, 63, 128, 134
Actors' Fund of America, The 13, 29, 135
Actors, The 8, 11, 23
Adams, Samuel Hopkins 78
Admirable Crichton, The 21
Al Hirschfeld Theatre, The 50
Alexander, Jane 163
Algonquin Hotel, The 23, 117, 164
Allen, Peter 7
Allen, Steve 103-113, 116, 119, 121, 122, 163
Allgood, Sara 56
Alwaleed, Prince 141, 142
American Born 60
American Musical Theater 63
American National Theatre & Academy, The 83, 85, 87
American Theater: A Chronicle of Comedy and Drama, 1869-1914 38
amNewYork 11, 12
Anderson, John 96
Anderson, Judith 21
Anglin, Margaret 75, 128
Archbold, Rick 44
Armstrong, Lil 68
Armstrong, Louis 67-71
Armstrong, Paul 128
Arsenic and Old Lace 82, 96, 97, 138
Askin, Harry 76, 77
Astor Hotel, The 22
Astor, John (Jacob) 44
Avian, Bob 91

Baby Cyclone, The 61
Bacon, Frank 42

Barrie, J.M. 21
Barrymore, Ethel 15, 17, 21, 24-27, 38, 64, 87, 128, 165
Barrymore, John 26, 27, 57, 64, 65
Barrymore, Lionel 21, 26, 64
Barrymore, Maurice 17, 26
Barum, Marcus 12
Bass, Paul 70
Bates, Blanche 40
Baxter, Ann 98
Bean, Judge Roy 31
Beck, Martin 50
Belasco Theatre, The 7, 20, 22, 25, 39, 52, 54, 101, 153, 159
Belasco, David 17, 39, 159
Bellamy, Ralph 128
Beloved Bandit, The 49, 72, 73
Beneath the Surface 136
Beng, Kwek Leng 8, 12, 138-141, 143, 144, 146, 147, 149, 150, 158
Benny, Jack 58, 119
Berlin, Irving 18, 66, 104, 105, 127, 130
Bernard, Sam 53
Beyond the Horizon 38
Billboard 113
Billie 61
Biltmore Los Angeles, The 145-147
Biltmore Theatre, The 128, 161
Blake, Betty 101
Bloomberg, Michael 94, 144
Blot in the 'Scutcheon, A 13, 29
Blue Ribbon Bar and Restaurant 8
Bogart, Humphrey 21, 81
Booth Theatre, The 39, 130
Bordman, Gerald 38
Born Yesterday 21
Brady, Jim 18
Brady, William A. 30
Breen, Robert 83-89, 91-95
Breen, Wilva 83-85, 87-89, 93, 95
Breese, Edmund 60

Brewster's Millions 13, 29
Brice, Fanny 21
Broadhurst Theatre, The 20, 22
Broadway Jones 61
Broadway Theatre, The 38
Broadway—Inside the Last Decade 101
Brown, Jared 57
Brown, John Mason 82
Bryan, David 165
Bull, William "Sitting" 19
Bundy, Laura Belle 119
Burke, Billie 21, 64
Burnett, Carol 130

Caban, Angela 152, 154
Café Pierre, The 93, 110, 111
Cahill, Lily 60
Calisauno, Lou 11
Calloway, Cab 68, 70
Cambridge, Godfrey 123
Capp, Al 112
Carnegie Pension Fund 126, 129
Carnegie, Andrew 15
Carpathia, The 45, 49
Carpenter, Edward Childs 42, 54
Carroll, Diahann 123
Carroll, Leo G. 98
Carson, Johnny 107, 108, 112, 117, 121
Caruso, Chuck 11
Caruso, Enrico 9, 17
Castle Garden Theatre, The 18
Cave Man, The 48
CBS Playhouse 77-79
Cerf, Bennett 78
Chagall, Marc 120
Chairman Kwek (see Beng, Kwek Leng)
Chapman, John 97
Chilton, Eleanor Carroll 82
Chinn, Everett 39
Chorus Line, A 91, 92
Christian Pilgrim, The 47
Christian Science Monitor, The 8, 11, 12
Chubbuck, Anne 12
Church's Cabaret 53
Ciacia, John "Cha-Cha" 105
Ciacia, Karen 105
Cinderella Man, The 17, 42, 54
Civitano, Tom 12
Clarence 53, 55-57, 64, 74, 98, 128
Cogan, David J. 128
Cohan, George M. 17, 27, 55, 58-66, 76, 133, 165
Cohan, Georgette 61
Collins, Ted 105

Columbia Broadcasting System (CBS) 77, 79, 105, 107, 112, 113, 116, 128, 130, 162
Columbia Theatre, The 30
Comley, Bonnie 12
Connie's Inn 68, 69
Considine, Bob 114
Cook, Barbara 163
Cordoba, Pedro de 60
Cornell, Katherine 65
Corrigan, Emmett 60
Cort Theatre, The 25
Count Basie 7
Cousin Kate 15, 24-27, 32, 38
Coward, Noël 118, 131
Coyle, Terence 137, 138
Crouse, Russel 19, 85, 92, 96, 98, 99, 109
Crudup, Arthur 113
Culinary Academy of New York, The 16
Cullen, Bill 111, 112
Cullman, Howard S. 109

DeFaa, Chip 58, 68
Dale, Frances 60
Dalrymple, Jean 166
Daly, Arnold 61
Danza, Tony 105
Davies, Hubert Henry 25
Davis, Bette 21
Davis, Miles 7
Davis, Richard Harding 30
DeBarr's Opera House 29
Delmonico's 23
Delmonico, Charley 17
Delsener, Ron 7, 88, 131-134
Detective Story, The 82, 99
Devlin, Jon 134
Diamond Lil 9
Diebel, Matt 12
Dilenschneider, Robert 12
Dinkins, David 163
Disney 20, 53, 165
Dodds, Johnny 68
Doll's House, A 21
Doyle, Arthur Conan 44
Dramatic Mirror, The 45, 47
Drew, John 26
Durst, Douglas 7
Durst, Seymour 7, 126, 129
Dwyer, William 126, 129

Ebersol, Christine 57
Edeson, Robert 49
Electra Chocolate Shop, The 53

Elliot, Maxine 17
Elmer the Great 61
Eltinge, Julian 25
Empire Theatre, The 25, 27, 40, 127
Etting, Ruth 77
Ewen, David 63

Fabulous Lunts, The 57
Fairbanks, Douglas 42
Fay, Larry 9
Feather, Leonard 69
Feinnes, Ralph 39
Feinstein, Michael 123
Feuerstein, Aron 136
Fields, Sidney 47
Fight, The 36, 50, 52, 53, 129
Filichia, Peter 135
Fiske, Minnie Madden 27, 28, 40, 41, 133, 154
Fitch, Clyde 128
Fitzgerald, Ella 108
Fitzgerald, John Francis 54
Flack, Roberta 7
Flanagan, Hallie 81
Fledgling 82
Foell, Earl 12
Folies Bergère Theatre, The 31, 48, 137, 138
Fonda, Jane 8, 124-126
Fontanne, Lynn 55, 56, 65, 74, 75, 98, 101, 131, 162
Force, Madeline Talmadge 44
Ford Theatre, The 32
Ford, Hugh 76
Francis, Arlene 123
Frank, Norman 114
Franklin, Joe 119, 120
Frankel, Aaron, 11
Friar's Club, The 61
Frick, Henry 15
Friendly Enemies 42, 53
Frohman, Charles 26, 27, 30, 40-42, 127
Frohman, David 20-22
Fulton Theatre, The 49, 96, 97, 137, 138
Fun I've Had, The 50
Futrelle, Jacques 44

Gaiety Theatre, The 9, 61
Gard, Alex 164
Garland, Robert 97
Gazarra, Ben 8, 125, 126
Genius and the Crowd 61
Gentlemen of the Press 39

George M. Cohan Theatre, The 60
Gerald Schoenfeld Theatre, The 91
Gershwin, George 66
Ghattas, Nadia 12
Gifford, Kathie Lee 165
Giles, Pressley 135
Gillespie, Dizzy 108
Gilsley House Hotel, The 18
Girl of the Golden West, The 39
Giuliani, Rudy 144
Goldberg, Whoopi 21
Goodman, Dody 122, 123
Goodrich, Arthur 60
Grand Opera House, The 49
Grant, Cary 96, 102
Grimaldi, John 12
Grisman, Sam H. 79
Gross, Jerry 28
Guditis, Helen 160-162
Guinan, Texas 9, 66
Guinan, Thomas 9

Hackett Theatre, The 30
Handman, Wynn 163, 164, 166
Hapgood, Norman 41
Hardee, Lewis 18, 22, 23
Hardy, Hugh 20
Harper, Leonard 68
Harris, Henry B. 13, 26, 29-32, 36, 37, 39-41, 44-46, 48-51, 57, 58, 61, 82, 127, 137, 158, 166
Harris, Irene 13, 88
Harris, Renee 23, 26, 37, 44-47, 49, 50, 54, 55, 57, 65, 72-74, 76, 79, 80, 81, 84
Harris, Rosemary 39
Harris, Sam H. 30, 58, 64
Harris, William 29, 30, 36, 50, 57
Hart, Kitty Carlisle 92-94
Hart, Moss 21, 49, 55, 65, 72, 73, 92
Harvard Club, The 23
Hasty Heart, The 96
Hayes, Helen 56, 65, 87, 98
Hearts Courageous 38
Held, Anna 17
Helen Hayes Theatre, The 20, 137, 138
Hellman, Lillian 124
Hellman, Per 12, 148, 155, 156, 158
Henderson, Skitch 106
Henry Miller Theatre, The 7, 36, 39
Hepburn, Katharine 81
Herbert, Victor 17, 18
Highly Personalized Guide to the Immediate Neighborhood, A 159
Hill, Edwin 77

Index 221

Hines, Elizabeth 61
Hingle, Pat 126
Hippodrome, The 18, 22, 39
Hirshfeld, Abraham 127
Hoadley, J.H. 45
Hoffman, Aaron 42, 53
Holliday, Judy 21, 121
Home Towners, The 60
Hong Leong Group, The 12, 140, 146
Hoogstraten, Nicholas Van 32
Horowitz, Jeffrey 136
Hot Chocolates 67-71
Hotel Commodore, The 18
Hotel Macklowe, The 133, 135, 136
Howard, Leslie 21, 81
Hudson Theatre Artists Guild, The 136
Hughes, John 12
Hulme, Emily 12
Huntington Theatre, The 28
Huston, Walter 21, 61, 101

If It Was Easy 12
Illington, Margaret 21, 22, 31
Immerman, Connie 68
Inside The Plaza 8
Irving, Henry Sir 26
Israels & Harder 35, 36

Jablonski Berkowitz Conservation, Inc 151
Jablonski, Mary 151
James, Aldon 130
James, John 130
Jazzlips Richardson and the Six Crackerjacks 69
Jefferson, Joseph 37, 40
Jenny Kissed Me 98
Jessel, George 77
Johnson, Kay 96
Jolivet, Rita 41
Jones, Clayton 12
Just Married 62

Kaplan, Justin 44
Karloff, Boris 11, 96, 97, 102
Karpov, Anatoly 135
Kasparov, Gary 135
Kaufman, George S. 21, 49, 65, 72, 117
Kerr, Jean 98
Kingsley, Sidney 99
Kirkland, Jack 79
Kissel, Howard 37
Klaw & Erlanger Theatrical Syndicate 30
Knickerbocker Hotel, The 17

Krembs, Felix 53
Kwek, Chairman (see Beng, Kwek Leng)

Lafayette Theater, The 69
Lambs Club 7, 8, 18, 20, 22, 23, 25, 61, 99, 128
Landis, Kathleen 93, 110
Landmarks Preservation Commission, The 33, 35, 76, 78, 88, 151
Lane, Stewart F. 12, 94, 160
Lang, George 12
Lange, Jessica 166
Langtry, Lily 31, 49
Lardner, Ring 61
Last Dinner on the Titanic 44
Lee, Beck 12
Legally Blond 94, 119
Lehren, Samuel 92
Lehrer, Samuel 128
Lemmon, Jack 38
Leshin, Phil, 11
Life With Father 19
Lincoln Center Theatre 21
Lind, Jenny 18
Lindsay, Howard 19, 20, 85, 92, 96, 98, 99, 109
Lindsay, Hudson 20
Lion and the Mouse, The 30, 31, 47
Lipskey, Seth 12
Little Nellie Kelly 61
Littler, Michael 158, 159
Long Voyage Home, The 38
Lord, Walter 54
Los Angeles 60
Loschiavo, LindaAnn 8, 9
Lost Broadway Theaters 32
Lunt, Alfred 55, 56, 65, 74, 75, 98, 128, 131, 162
Lure, The 51, 52
Lusitania, The 27, 41
Lyceum Theatre, The 9, 21, 22, 25, 27, 31, 40, 127, 162
Lyons, Jimmy 111
Lyric Theatre, The 20

MacArthur, Charles 98
MacDonald, Christie 17
MacHugh, Augustin 58
Macklowe, Harry 132, 134, 135, 138, 143
MacLaine, Shirley 38
Madden, Owney 8
Madeleine and the Movies 61
Maggie Pepper 29

Majestic Theatre, The 20, 22, 38
Mann, Louis 53
Mansfield, Richard 41
Mantle, Burns 98
Marcin, Max 60
Marlowe, Joan 101
Marques, Stuart 12
Marriott Marquis Hotel, The 137, 138
Martin Beck Theatre, The 50
Martin, Mary 11
Martin, Vivian 62
Martini, Nino 77
Massey, Raymond 97, 102
Masterson, William "Bat" 17
Matinee Tomorrow 28
McAdoo, William 51, 52
McCaulay, Dana 44
McCormick, Myron 96
McElfatrick & Son 36
McGurn, Barbara 12
McKay, Andy 107
McMahon, Ed 107
McMahon, Horace 99
McWade, Robert 60
Meadows, Jane 111
Meanest Man in the World, The 58, 63
Menil, Francois de 132, 134
Mercer, Mabel 111
Merrick, David 37
Merry Malones, The 61
Metz, Robert 105, 106, 122
Millennium & Copthorne Hotels 8, 146
Millennium Hotels and Resorts 8, 12, 13, 39, 54, 95, 108, 120, 133, 139, 140, 142-145, 147-151, 155, 156, 158
Mills, Irving 17
Minskoff Theatre, The 20
Moore, Victor 17
Morasco Theatre, The 138
Morehouse, Elizabeth 12
Morehouse, Ward 8, 23, 24, 28, 39, 59, 63, 66, 74, 76, 77, 96, 98, 99, 104, 119, 127, 164
Morehouse, William 12
Morris, Chester 60
Morrison, Craig 35, 36
Morrison, Priestly 73
Moss, Bob 161
Musetto, Vincent 12
Music Box Theatre, The 104, 127, 130

Nania, John 12
Nash, Ogden 108
National Actors Theatre 21
National Arts Society Urban Center, The 36
National Broadcasting Company, The (NBC) 92, 93, 104, 105, 108, 109, 111, 113-115, 117, 118, 120, 122, 128, 129
National Producing Managers of America 13
National Theatre Foundation, The 85, 86, 94
Nemesis 60
New Amsterdam Roof, The 42, 79
New Amsterdam Theatre, The 9, 20, 25, 27, 79, 162
New Haven Register, The 26
New Lyceum Theatre, The 20
New Victory Theatre, The 9, 27, 36
New York Daily News, The 47, 97, 132
New York Herald Tribune, The 70
New York Herald, The 62
New York Journal-American, The 96, 97
New York magazine 134
New York Post, The 7, 11, 12, 82, 114, 124, 125
New York Shakespeare Festival, The 91, 92
New York Sun, The 11, 12, 24, 70, 76, 77, 98
New York Theatre, The 9
New York Times, The 8, 32, 40, 41, 51, 52, 56, 70, 85, 129
New York World-Telegram, The 79
New York Yacht Club, The 23
Newsday 151
Newsweek magazine 107
Night at the Opera, A 94
Night to Remember, A 54
Nixon, Cynthia 28
Nixon, Richard 116
Nokia Rock Theatre, The 20
Noose, The 49
Nugent, Eliot 61
Nye, Louis 108

O'Casey, Sean 56
O'Casey, Siobhan 56
O'Neill, Eugene 38, 40, 65, 66, 81, 95, 99-101, 124-126, 138
O'Neill, James 37
Oh! Calcutta! 7
Okeh Records 68
Olympia Theatre, The 22
Origlio, Tony 12
Ory, "Kid" 68
Osmond, Donny 165
Other Girl, The 21
Overman, Lynne 62

Paar, Jack 103, 104, 107-109, 112-123, 163
Page, Geraldine 124, 125, 126
Palace Theatre, The 81
Papert, Fred 160
Papp, Joseph 88, 91, 92, 138
Parenteau, Gail 12
Patrick, John 96
Pearman, Jared 12
Peter Pan 11
Phoenix Repertory Company, The (APA) 21
Pinos, Dina 12
Plaza, The 12, 39, 120, 140-142
Plough and the Stars, The 56
Porter, Cole 65
Porterfield, Bob 85
Presley, Elvis 106, 107, 113, 163
Prince, William 126
Proud Prince, The 21

Quintero, José 125

Ragavan, Sudheer 156
Rahe, Roderic 11
Randall, Tony 21, 112, 114
Ray, Randolph 23
Rayburn, Gene 112
Razaf, Andy 67, 68, 70, 71
Rector's 8
Rehan, Ada 17
Republic Theatre, The 27, 36
Reuters 11, 20, 93
Revere, Ann 124
Reynolds, Joey 112, 121
Rich, Frank 8, 11
Richard, Charles J. 30
Rickman, Alan 165
Riskin, Martin 12, 120
Robards, Jason 124, 135
Roberts, Doris 166
Roddy, Rod 112
Roderick, David M. 90
Rogers, Will 41, 43
Roosevelt, Theodore 17
Rosenthal, Craig 12
Rothstein, Arnold 67
Royale Theatre, The 9
Russell, Lillian 17

Santana, Carlos 7
Sardi's 164
Sarnoff, Bob 115
Savoy, The 132-134, 165

Scanlan, Eugene 12
Scarecrow, The 48
Schoenfeld, Gerald 130
Schreiber, Terry 125
Schultz, Dutch 67, 68, 70, 71
Scott, Vernon 114
Seelan, Roseane 136
Seldes, Marian 163
Shakespeare, William 37, 95, 136
Shanley's 8, 16-18
Shanley, Patrick 18
Shanley, Peter 18
Shanley, Robert C. 16
Shanley, Tom 16
Shapiro, Gary 12
Sheldon, Edward 27
Shepard, Sam 164, 166
Shipman, Samuel 42, 53
Show Business 129, 130
Show Shop, The 42
Shubert Archive, The 22
Shubert Theatre, The 20, 22, 38, 91, 92, 127
Shubert, Lee 51, 52, 64
Shuberts, The 21, 89, 130
Simms, Margaret 70
Sinclair, Arthur 56
Sitomer, Curt 11
Skipworth, Alison 60
Smith, Edward J. 44
Smith, Kate 104, 105
Smith, Leroy 69
So This Is London 60
Soldiers of Fortune 30
Song and Dance Man, The 60-63, 66
Spalding, Albert 77
St. Cyr, Johnny 68
St. James Theatre, The 20, 22
Stage in America (1897-1900), The 41
Stahl, Rose 29
Stanwyck, Barbara 49
Stapleton, Maureen 124
State of the Union 82, 96-98
Steuer, Max D. 51, 52
Stewart, Donald Ogden 60
Stonehill & Taylor 147, 148, 151, 155
Storizinski, Alex 12
Strange Interlude 8, 124, 125
Sulka, Arlie 151
Sweikert, Gary 12

Tarkington, Booth 55-57, 64, 128
Taubman, Howard 124
Tavern, The 60, 61
Taylor, Charles A. 38

Taylor, Paul 148
Templeton, Fay 17
Theater Critics Review 11
Theater Information Bulletin, The 11, 101
Theater Managers' Association of Greater New York 13, 29
Theater Weekly 135
Theatre Museum, The 36, 94, 155, 160-163
Theatrical Syndicates 40, 41
Thief, The 21
Thomas, Augustus 30, 60, 65
Thomas, Frank M. 58
Thomas, Richard 125
Through Fire and Water 38
Tiffany & Company 33, 151, 152, 154-156
Time magazine 37
TimesSquare.com 11
Titanic, The 13, 26, 29, 41, 44-47, 49, 54, 79, 127
Tone, Franchot 125, 126
Tonight Show, The 105, 122
Toys in the Attic 124
Travel Smart Newsletter, 11
Troupe Theatre, The 11

Un, Deux, Trois 39
Underhill, Paul 12, 142-144, 150
United Press International 114
United States Steel 90, 93, 126, 129
Unter, Bob 115

Valentino, Rudolph 9
Variety 70, 129
Veiller, Bayard 36, 37, 50
Vig, Joel 119

Wagner, Robert F. 128
Waldorf-Astoria, The 12, 111, 120, 155, 158
Waller, Fats 68, 70, 71
Walnut Street Theatre, The 49
Walter, Eugene 38, 65
Waring, Richard 23
Watson, Lucile 128
Watson, Minor 96
Watts, Richard 11
Watts, Richard Jr. 124, 125
Webber, Andrew Lloyd 38
West, Mae 9
Wexler, Warren 120
Wheeler, Hugh 128
When the Actors Owned New York 44
Whispering Friends 60
Sally Button White, 11
White, Stanford 22
Whitehead, Robert 128
Widow Jones, The 30
Wilder, Alec 111
Wilkie, Wendell 98
Wilson, Earl 114
Wilson, Edith 69, 70
Wilson, Julie 123
Wilson, Mary Louise 57
Wilson, Woodrow 17
Winchell, Walter 164
Winsome Widow, A 9
Within the Law 50
Wolf, Lillian Kramer 164
Wolf, William 164
Wooding, Russell 69
Woods, A.H. 30, 42, 53, 64
Woodward, Joanne 163, 164
Woollcott, Alexander 56, 61, 62, 77, 78, 117
Worth, Irene 124
Wynn, Steve 141

Ziegfeld Midnight Frolic, The 53
Ziegfeld, Florenz 30, 64, 79
Zolotow, Sam 129

www.ingramcontent.com/pod-product-compliance
Lightning Source LLC
Chambersburg PA
CBHW071436150426
43191CB00008B/1147